Praise for *What If Anger Is the Answer?*

"We live in a plastic age, physically and spiritually. Mike LeBlanc takes us back to the wisdom of the ancients, and reminds us why some things have mattered through the ages: honor, virtue, nobility, and—yes—anger. I love this book."

—Nate Fick, *New York Times* Bestselling Author,
One Bullet Away

"We live in a time hungry for virtue—and flooded with its imitations. This book is about the real thing."

—Steven Pressfield, *New York Times* Bestselling Author,
The War of Art and *Gates of Fire*

"I've watched Mike grow as a leader in Afghanistan, in building his companies, and in raising a family. This book is a rare look at how to do those things well."

—Lt. Col. Thomas Schueman, USMC,
Bestselling Author, *Always Faithful*

"This book addresses a rarely discussed element of leadership: Anger, when disciplined, is not a flaw but a signal that honor and responsibility are still alive."

—Lt. Gen. George Smith Jr., US Marines (Ret),
Founder and CEO, BROADSWORD Leadership

What If Anger Is the Answer?

What If Anger Is the Answer?

A HARVARD MARINE'S GUIDE TO SHAPING AGGRESSION

MIKE LeBLANC

MATT HOLT

Matt Holt Books
An Imprint of BenBella Books, Inc.
Dallas, TX

The events, locations, and conversations in this book, while true, are re-created from the author's memory. However, the essence of the story and the feelings and emotions evoked are intended to be accurate representations. In certain instances, names, persons, organizations, and places have been changed to protect an individual's privacy.

The views expressed in this publication are those of the author and do not necessarily reflect the official policy or position of the Department of War or the U.S. government. The public release clearance of this publication by the Department of War does not imply Department of War endorsement or factual accuracy of the material

MATT HOLT BENBELLA

Matt Holt is an imprint of BenBella Books, Inc.
8080 N. Central Expressway
Suite 1700
Dallas, TX 75206
benbellabooks.com
Send feedback to feedback@benbellabooks.com

Printed in the United States of America
10 9 8 7 6 5 4 3 2 1

Library of Congress Control Number: 2026938720
ISBN 9781637749227 (hardcover)
ISBN 9781637749234 (electronic)

Copyediting by Michael Fedison
Proofreading by Lisa Story, Marissa Wold Uhrina, and Denise Pangia
Text design and composition by Jordan Koluch
Printed by Lake Book Manufacturing

To Chiryze, Michael, Claire, and Ellie

Contents

PART III: CYNICISM AND COHERENCE

PART IV: BUILDING IN A BROKEN WORLD

To My Son

It seems like the further you go back in history, the easier it was to become a man. Before civilization, you couldn't stay a boy if you wanted to survive. You couldn't live without learning to hunt, kill, and avoid dangers. You ate what you killed, owned what you earned, and found your place with others by giving, sharing, and protecting. In a world of scarcity and life-threatening danger everywhere, you had to grow up fast.

In today's world, it's more difficult. You've had a bed to sleep in since the day you were born. You've never had to track an animal to eat. You were born into a whole world of things you didn't build. These days, if you watch football, change your oil, and grill chicken, you might as well be Paul Bunyan.

A lot of people, seeing how far civilization has come,

think that it doesn't matter whether you're a man in the old sense anymore. They wish that men would stop being so aggressive, obstinate, stubborn, and stupid. They roll their eyes at the ones who beat their chests.

For a while, I agreed with that. I grew up in working-class Ohio, where everyone made money with their hands and backs. They were plumbers, electricians, and builders. They worked with wood, stone, and concrete. My dad painted houses for over 50 years.

But when I moved to Maryland for college, I felt like I was entering a new and refined world. The boats in Annapolis cost more than my parents' house. It seemed like I'd gone from blue collar to blue blood. I pictured myself like someone in a movie, a member of the aristocracy and ruling class. Someone who read books and had a favorite kind of brandy.

I felt proud to be in high society. The people there talked about jibs and juxtaposed things. I needed a dictionary to keep up. They played croquet and sniffed wine before they sipped it. I loved it. Who needed a world where men fought and worked with their hands? It was God's small mercy that I didn't know where to buy a seersucker suit.

As part of my new life, I started to translate Ancient Greek and dedicated myself to exploring the classics. I was sure at the time that studying the Great Books would only confirm the high-minded ideas I was cultivating. Although the Naval Academy was just across the street, I expected to learn all the best arguments against war and barbarism.

Instead, Plato and Aristotle and the other Ancients taught the opposite. They taught how to shape anger and aggression. The Greeks wouldn't scoff at gym class; they thought sports were critical to the development of young men. They wouldn't look at the eighteen-year-olds enlisting in the military with pity, nor blame their patriotism as unthinking; they insisted that men train for wars and fight courageously in them. The Greeks didn't medicate aggression away or suppress anger. They weren't worried about boys who couldn't sit still or by young men angry at the world.

Those don't seem to be the standard positions anymore. The ancient attitudes toward aggression and strife awoke in me a sort of anger when I learned of them; I felt I'd been lied to by the modern world. The modern world wanted me to believe that happiness was a matter of pleasure-seeking. They wanted me to choose balance over excellence. They wanted me to treat all anger as a negative emotion. They frowned on my hope for glory. They wanted me trained as a good employee. They cared much less about who I was as a husband, as a leader, or as a father.

Studying the Great Books, I suddenly felt like I had to reject the comfortable civilization I'd grown up in. I was ashamed that I was so soft, even ashamed that my parents had loved me so much and brought me up so well. I longed for adversity, challenges, and tests of my mettle. That was one of the main reasons I signed up to become a Marine and go to war. The Marine Corps offered a stark contrast to the entitled and comfortable world, and helped me solidify lessons I wouldn't have otherwise understood.

The quick version of what I learned is this: *Although you don't need to go to war to become a man, a warlike mentality is critical.* A warlike mentality encompasses many principles, but among them are these:

1. Accept indisputable facts quickly, no matter how bad.
2. Locate, close with, and destroy the enemy, whoever or whatever the enemy is.
3. Be a happy warrior and fight with optimism.

Our world still provides plenty of opportunity for grit, ambition, and manliness, but they won't come to you if you don't look for them. There's nothing wrong with making money or being rich, so long as you still get scars and calluses from working for them. Finally, and most importantly, it's natural and good for you to want to compete and be the best, but there's a right way to win.

Warlike is an obsolete word that's rarely used, not because we've come up with a new word, but because we've stopped believing in the idea it represents. We no longer have a word for focused, offensive aggression that seeks conflict and victory. Yet understanding that kind of anger and making use of it has long been the most important education for a young man.

I've told you and your sisters forever that I'm not a perfect man and that everybody makes mistakes. You'll find that this book is an encyclopedia of mistakes I've made—and they're just the ones I'm willing to tell! I've always loved the part of the movie where the hero is learning his skills, including all the missteps and early iterations. These are mine.

I've tried to capture how funny everything was, because, although we were dealing with death and serious things, there's no way to get through the tough times without laughing at the absurdities. I hope that you can learn from these stories. They certainly taught me a thing or two and maybe they can help you avoid having to learn everything the hard way.

Grandpa John always said to me growing up, "I'm so proud of the man you're turning yourself into." Now, as I watch you grow up in turn, I can't help but think the same thing every day. I hope you never have to go to a real war. But in the battles that will be yours to fight as you become a man, I hope this book might help you win.

Love,
Dad

Part I

ME AGAINST THE WORLD

Chapter 1

THE ANGEL, THE DEVIL, AND THE CHIP ON YOUR SHOULDER

NOT A WAR STORY

We were eating goat for lunch again. Staff Sergeant Williams and I were at the Afghan Army chow hall, a large tent that managed to feel like an elementary school field trip to Afghanistan. I smiled in conversation with the Afghan soldiers, moving the goat around on my plate to look like I was eating.

Gunshots. This time from just a few tables away. Afghan soldiers ran out of the chow hall, some screaming. Chaos erupted all round, as though a starter pistol had gone off. Everywhere was confusion. Had someone's weapon gone off by accident? Not likely with multiple shots. Could the Taliban have gotten in? If they had, we would have heard machine-gun fire. Were there other Marines in the chow hall? Were Williams and I the targets?

Williams's rifle was up. Unconsciously, I found myself mirroring his actions. He moved professionally through the crowd toward the gunfire. He wasn't confused or frantic. He was calm and determined. He moved with authority. I followed close behind, glad that Williams was there to set the example.

We saw an Afghan soldier down on the ground, bloody and surrounded by other soldiers. They waved for us to come over. Williams broke through and took charge. The Afghan had been shot in the head, his face covered in blood. But he was still breathing.

Although I technically outranked Williams, in this situation I was relieved to see him take charge. "Sir," he called to me. "Hold his head right here. Don't let it come apart. I'm calling for medical." He immediately radioed for a truck to get the wounded man to the doctors.

"Can we save him?" I asked hopefully, holding the soldier's face together as he gasped for air.

"He was shot in the face," Williams said in a tone that suggested it was a stupid question. "No chance."

The truck backed in within minutes and some of the Afghans helped us load the soldier into the back. As we sped down the desert road, Williams hooked up an IV. The bullet had come at such an angle that it split the soldier's face in half.

As we'd loaded him up, we learned over the radio that the shooter was another Afghan soldier, and that he'd already been taken into custody. It turned out that the two had been rivals, in love with the same girl back home. It had nothing to do with the war. Nothing to do with our mission, Islam, or the Taliban. It was the unsurprising result of having given guns to teenagers.

I held the soldier's face together as best I could, but I was only juggling irretrievably broken pieces. It seemed to me that's what this war was—just a bloody mess that I was trying to shape into a face. No one thought we'd win this war. We were just rushing a dead patient to a doctor.

Every soldier who'd been in the chow hall was used to getting shot at on patrol, but when it came during lunch, they screamed and ran away from the attack. No one raced toward the gunfire but Williams.

Being on my team was a sort of exile for Williams. He was from Marine Recon, an elite unit I hoped to join someday. This was his sixth deployment in the 10 years he'd been a Marine. He was tactically and technically a complete professional, but had a habit of getting into trouble. Flying in through Kyrgyzstan, Williams had gotten drunk, hit on a female superior officer, and tried to get me to fight him.

Growing up, people didn't think Williams would amount to much, which made him angry. What made him angrier is he knew they were probably right. He was angry that he'd been born to a bad family in a bad neighborhood. That he didn't have any opportunities and felt he didn't deserve them anyway.

At 18, Williams brought all his raw anger and frustration

to the Marine Corps where he took it out on himself and everyone around him. He got into fights, but he also put himself through the toughest training he could find. He was drown-proofed in the water, training that included blacking out in the pool under supervision. Daily, he ran with a full flak jacket and rifle, wearing a mask to restrict his oxygen. He used shame as a tool to shape his soul.

Today, though, Williams seemed anything but a screwup. While everyone else was in a story they'd tell the rest of their lives, Williams looked like he was checking into another day at the office. He didn't hesitate, weaving expertly through the crowd, prepared to respond to any threat. The anger that had once come out in drunkenness and picking fights was now manifest in something focused and noble.

ANGER, OBVIOUSLY, ISN'T THE ANSWER

I'd always been told that anger wasn't the answer to anything. Rage was like alcohol but without any fun. The pattern was always the same. Drunk with anger, I'd make bad decisions. Once my anger subsided, my rational self was left with a hangover of apologies and regret. Anger was bad for kids, bad for work, and bad for marriage. It seemed pretty simple.

But when I started studying Greek philosophy, I found that they had a whole different take. Aristotle counted proper anger as virtuous. Too much anger, he said, was exactly the temper tantrum I'd thought it was. But he also said it was a vice, a moral failing, to not get angry enough. For him, the virtue of anger meant being mad at the right time toward the right person to the right degree.

It made sense as I thought about it. I remembered back to the first time I was ever punched in the face. I didn't get angry. I just stood there, dumbfounded, while my friend defended me, punching the other guy out. Aristotle wouldn't have been surprised that my angry friend was greeted as a hero back in the classroom. We aren't evolved to watch a bear attack our family and marvel at the food chain. We're supposed to get angry, to shut down our merely selfish interests. We're built to jump in front of our kids and sacrifice our lives to kill the bear.

I was even more surprised when I read Socrates's account of anger. In Plato's *Republic*, he went even further than saying proper anger was virtuous. He said that anger was an essential part of the soul. Shaping and developing our anger was an indispensable part of living a good life. His story of anger in the soul became a sort of mystery for me, one that I'd spend years of my life figuring out.

I'm going to share his account here, but let me warn you up front that it's strange. Aristotle's idea of proper anger wasn't too difficult to grasp. You shouldn't get too angry, but you need to get angry enough. Socrates isn't so straightforward. In locating anger's place in the soul, he concocts a weird metaphor in which our souls have *three* parts:

- a small man, who represents our mind and reasoning
- a hydra, a many-headed beast that stands for our appetites
- and a lion, which embodies our anger and everything to do with our sense of self-worth

All three of these characters—the small man, the hydra, and the lion—live together in one human body. It's a cage match.

To think of my mind as a small, rational man and my appetites as a many-headed monster made good sense to me straightaway. Life often felt like a battle between the rational and irrational, between my mind and my body. Everyone understands why cartoons put an angel on one shoulder and a devil on the other. The devil suggests that we hit the next casino while the angel tells us it's time for bed. Everyone has internal debates between the angel and devil.

When we resist the chocolate cake and ask for the check instead, we let the angel guide us toward a healthy, sensible life. When we decide that the cake and Crème brûlée both look too good to pass up, the devil leads us into self-indulgence and corruption. One trip to go people-watching at the mall is enough to reveal what a skilled debater the devil is.

Socrates's small man plays the part of the angel on your shoulder. His hydra plays the part of the devil. Already, with a hydra posed against a small man, it's clear that the smart money won't be on rational thought. For Socrates, life wasn't an even fight between good and evil. Evil had all but won the fight before they even got in the ring.

What really confused me, though, was why Socrates added the third part. *Good and evil aren't enough?*, I wondered. Even more confusing was that the third part included anger. If one head of the monster was greed, another lust, and so on, wasn't anger clearly one of those heads? What could be more devilish or monstrous than anger? To make it even more of a mystery, Socrates's picture of anger's source wasn't a rabid dog or a fire. It was a lion—a noble, regal animal.

PEANUT BUTTER

I didn't really start to understand why Socrates had a third part in the soul until I'd finished a hard training course called the Infantry Officer Course (IOC) in the Marines. IOC was about pushing your body to the limit. We'd go without food and without sleep. We'd run 20 miles one day then carry 200-pound packs the next. It was brutal. After I graduated from the course, I felt entitled to a reward. Just after IOC ended, I went to Virginia Beach to attend a relaxed classroom course. For three months, I'd get eight hours of sleep each night in a hotel room and could eat whatever I wanted. On my first night before class, I bought loads of junk food—chips, ice cream, and my personal favorite, peanut butter. I hadn't eaten any of those in months, so I turned on the TV and let my hydra go wild.

I opened the jar of peanut butter and took out a spoonful. Then another. And another. Soon, I was feeling a bit sick from all the crap I'd eaten, but it seemed I could always fit another bite of peanut butter. About halfway through the jar, eating the peanut butter stopped being fun. I was sickened with myself. Even more revolting than the peanut butter was the debate I was having with myself. I could feel Socrates's parts discussing the situation:

Small Man (the mind): You really shouldn't be eating all this peanut butter. Do you know how many calories are in a jar?

Hydra (the appetites): Calories?! [Takes another bite.] Screw you! Where was the calorie-counting when you starved me for the past 10 weeks?!

Small Man (the mind): That's a fair point. I suppose you're entitled to a little freedom . . .

Hydra (the appetites): You treat me like your slave! Now it's my turn, moron!

[*Takes another bite.*]

It went on this way for about an hour, until the peanut butter jar was empty. I was exhausted, sick, and still reached for more snacks.

Hydra (the appetites): How about something salty . . .

Small Man (the mind): I really think we should start thinking about bed. It's past midnight and our course starts at 6 AM.

Hydra (the appetites): Chips! Perfect! [Starts eating chips.]

Small Man (the mind): I guess a few more won't kill you, but this is the last snack.

[*Eats more.*]

Finally, my third part stepped in.

Lion (anger): Enough! The two of you are disgusting! You just became an infantry officer in the United States Marine Corps, and you can't stop yourself from eating junk food? Hydra, you're like a revolting child with no discipline. Small Man, you're like a weak parent who wonders why his kid keeps acting out. We're putting our shoes on right now.

Hydra (the appetites): I don't want to put any shoes on.

Small Man (the mind): We should really get some sleep before class tomorrow, Lion.

Lion (anger): Shut up! Shoes on. Now! We're going on a run.

With that, I forced myself outside to run for 10 miles in the middle of the night. By 2 AM, I was completely wiped. The next morning, as I began my first day in the classroom only four hours later, I had bags under my eyes and my face was bloated. Everyone could see that I was wrecked from the night before. "Looks like Virginia Beach gave you quite a welcome," one of my buddies said. They all imagined me partying, drinking, and spending the night with the college kids on spring break. I felt pathetic and ashamed.

After that night, as embarrassed as I felt, I realized that I had a new puzzle piece to help me understand Socrates's lion. Anger was more than just a protective behavior. The lion is the part of us that can become disgusted with ourselves. When we can't stand watching our appetites overrule our minds, anger is what steps in to help set things straight. When we can get the mind and anger to work together, we tip the scales toward reason. This is why Aristotle says that shame is almost a virtue. When we're able to feel disgusted with ourselves, we're also in a position to start some self-discipline.

To most people, the lion seems about as savage and monstrous as the hydra, leaving reason next to no chance against both. Merely suppressing anger looks like chopping off a hydra head; the monster simply grows another one somewhere else. But Socrates showed another way. If we can get our lion to become an ally of the small man, if we can somehow couple our anger with reason, we may perhaps unlock a harmony or fellowship in the soul. Getting the lion properly trained and educated was his path to a good and beautiful life. As I worked on understanding what he laid out, I discovered that curbing my passion for peanut butter was just the tip of the iceberg.

COMFORT-BASED DECISIONS

I'd always liked the idea of sculpting my soul, but I'd never thought about how painful that might be for the block of marble. I may have framed the project as Me Against the World, but it turned out that Me needed a lot of work.

At Officer Candidate School (OCS)—boot camp for Marines who had graduated from college—pleasure was a bad reason to do anything. Any complaint about harsh conditions was whining. Attempts to ease pain were called comfort-based decisions. They weren't to be made. You couldn't stop a march on the enemy because you were hungry, or give in to sleep because you were tired from patrolling all day. Comfort-based decisions would kill your Marines. I hadn't been to war yet, but that seemed to make sense.

I cared a lot less about what sense it made, though, when

I was freezing, hungry, and exhausted. I'd expected to be above those sorts of pains and discomforts. Before going to OCS, it seemed absurd that I'd consider altering a committed life plan over such things. But face-to-face with the actual hardships, it was a different story. My only unqualified pleasures at OCS were three 10-minute meals in the day and the few moments at night when I could read letters from home.

The sergeant instructors would rail against us for how happy we were when we got our letters or got to eat. "Snacks and mail, right?!" they'd scream. "I thought I had a bunch of candidates who wanted to lead Marines! I thought I had candidates who came here because they were sick of being fat civilians! That they wanted to be here to learn how they could protect their Marines from dying. But nooooo! You just came here for the snacks and mail!"

I recalled what I'd read in Aristotle's *Ethics*, a book that addresses what it means to live a good life. He identifies three primary motivations: pleasure, honor, and wisdom. Most people, he says, focus on pleasure-seeking. They spend their lives trying to maximize their fun, living under the motto "eat, drink, and be merry." When I read his description of such people, I resisted its relevance to me. I hated to think that I might fall into that camp.

Aiming at virtue and honor felt like a much better fit. As far as I could see, the pleasure-seekers had to wonder whether their lives would ever add up to anything, ever mean anything serious. They were doomed to look back from their deathbeds, afraid that they hadn't done or built anything worthwhile. Those on the honor team might not die comfortably in their beds, but at least they were saved from that other worry.

At OCS, I started to wonder whether I'd understood the *Ethics* right. The life I lived at OCS—marching through rain and snow, holding a rifle with stiff, cold hands, staring at the shaved head in front of me—didn't seem much like a life that added up to much. As I marched in those ranks, I calculated how many minutes of my day I didn't dread. The hydra suddenly looked like it deserved another chance, a better hearing. I had to admit I really liked the snacks and mail.

I'd thought that an excellent human life needed to be serious and disciplined. Up close, the serious life I'd chosen started to look like not much of a life at all. I didn't want to become a robotic soldier with a shaved head and no interest in ice cream. Excellence needed room for fun, pleasure, and friends.

TOO SMART FOR ANGER

With my mind in charge, I felt above dying for my country—too smart to take those risks and too good to dirty my hands. I felt like Shakespeare's Hamlet.

Hamlet seems to have the makings of a great king. He's conscientious and smart. If he were running for Congress, you might vote for him. His father was a strong king who'd protected his kingdom by defeating a challenger in single combat, defending his crown with his sword. Hamlet seems to have a similar strength, but he's more intellectual than his father. He's a student of religion, government, and philosophy.

But we don't see Hamlet gracefully taking over from his father. Instead, his father is murdered by his own brother, Claudius. Thereafter, Claudius becomes king and marries Hamlet's mother. Hamlet is called home from university and faces a terrible decision: kill his uncle Claudius in vengeance for his father's murder or keep the peace and spare his mother from the shame and horror. There's no good answer to his situation. Although Hamlet is inclined toward revenge, he can't stop second-guessing himself.

Initially, the nub of the play appears to be a test of wits: How can Hamlet unseat the king, save his mother, and restore uncorrupted rule to Denmark? But that's not the deepest issue. In the course of the play, Hamlet in fact gets all the evidence he needs to have Claudius legitimately deposed as king. The central problem with Hamlet is less a matter of thinking too much than one of thinking too little of his anger, shame, and outrage. In his puritanical aloofness, he looks down on his heart.

Justice and revenge call for Hamlet to act, but he achieves no resolve. His heart says kill, while his mind says stay pure. He feels above revenge. He feels too good for rage. He feels too smart for his own conflict. Hamlet is at war with himself, in spiritual disarray. Without alignment in his soul he can't act, let alone rule.

THE LION EMERGES

Part of what made OCS so difficult was that I wanted it to be difficult. I was so excited to take on challenges that I'd make things harder than they needed to be. In our Meals-Ready-to-Eat, I'd skip the dessert. When my mind would put up red flags for safety, I'd push harder, running faster when my knees started to hurt or holding out a few more seconds when someone had me in an arm bar.

One of the most important things I had to learn was that you don't get extra credit for struggling. I'd been letting my ambition run roughshod over my mind and appetites. And it was catching up with me.

We were training in the snow and we were freezing when a white van pulled up. Two men with medium fade haircuts were inside. They weren't sergeant instructors; they were captains. They didn't scream. We rarely got to talk to them, but one of them jumped out and approached a small group of us.

"How you doing, gentlemen?" he asked. Looking us up and down a moment, he shook his head.

"Good evening, sir!" we yelled in unison, misreading the situation.

"You don't need to do all that," he said. "Have a seat." We sat down on our camp stools, shivering. "Guys," he said, reasoning with us. "This is stupid. I know you're all clenching your fists and gritting your teeth, thinking that if you can just get through these 10 weeks, you'll be good. But this isn't some obstacle between you and being a Marine—it's the life of a Marine. It's not glamorous. It's miserable."

Like Milton's Satan, his words weren't the devilish lies I was expecting; they were persuasive and reasonable. He was speaking all of my own worries to me: This might not be the test but the reality.

"There's no shame in dropping," he continued, sipping what looked like hot coffee. "Good on you for sticking it out until now. But you're not better than the guys who've dropped. They just realized this wasn't for them. They just realized that they didn't feel like spending their lives cold and hungry. If you drop right now, nothing dramatic happens." He looked over at the van, still running while the other instructor looked at his phone in the passenger's seat. "You just go into that warm van and hang out with us. We've even got an extra burrito."

My stomach started making noises, ordering me to get in the van. He was right that it felt stupid. Guys dropped voluntarily every day. At least today, you got a burrito. Still, I didn't move.

"I'm all good, sir," I said, chiming in with the other candidates, all of us putting on a brave face. The instructor gave us a last look and shrugged, shaking his head again as he climbed back into the cozy van.

I'd aspired to be above mundane desires. I liked to think I could just decide to overcome and overrule them. But I'd been treating them like slaves, and now I suspected rebellion. I was at war with myself. I'd imagined that I was undertaking a glorious enterprise to train and shape my heart and will. I'd assumed it meant chaining appetite and overriding selfish calculations.

Here, though, it was starting to look like a far bigger project than I'd signed up for. Right now, my stomach was the adversary—and it was proving to be a worthy one. I'd thought that my mind would be a natural ally in my fight against desires. But in the eternal fight between spirit and flesh, reason could be a mercenary, backing whichever side it predicted would win.

It was the lion that was keeping me from giving up. The small man of the mind and my hydra each saw in their own way that eating when you're hungry is good. They didn't give a damn what was beautiful! The lion was the part of me that knew there was something else worth defending. Others might see that resistance as stubborn or unreasonable, but Plato had gotten it just right. If you want a good life, the small man can certainly help; if you want a beautiful one, you'd better understand the lion. Anyone who has accepted a dare understands what this dimension of the soul feels like. It's the space of peer pressure, of honor, of distinction. It's why someone might cheat at a board game, and why all of us can get so angry when we lose.

I had to understand that strengthening my will wasn't just an exercise of defiance, but one of integration as well. I wasn't supposed to silence the body or override reason. I needed my mind, appetite, and ambition to become friends with each other, rather than struggle for brute domination.

Practically speaking, making my different elements friends didn't look like anything out of the ordinary. I started eating the desserts when I had them and accepted invites to go out drinking with the other Marines when the course was over. When my knees hurt, I'd slow down.

The big change came in the way I was telling my story to myself. Instead of writing my own epic, where every episode gave me impossible odds to survive, I started telling myself, "It's not *that* bad." That became a sort of mantra for me. When I was exhausted, it was easy to spiral, worrying about how much worse the exhaustion would get. But when I really thought about my pain at any given moment, I could honestly say, "It's not *that* bad." When I had an opportunity to ease things, I didn't race to it like I was grabbing onto a lifesaver, but I would accept it, knowing that it didn't take away from my win.

In our hand-to-hand combat training, "body hardening" consisted of punching trees over and over in order to build calluses. I had been doing a version of that with everything in my life. But at graduation, they didn't give extra credit to those who struggled the most. The more I figured out how to be a friend to myself, the easier and more satisfying the wins seemed to get.

THE WISDOM OF ATHENS

The Ancient Greeks had a different word for this center of anger, aggression, and disgust: *thumos. Thumos* is a primal and instinctive part of us, but it can serve higher ends. It's the willingness to die in a fight when someone insults you, but also what allows you to risk your life for your family. *Thumos* is the unity that lies behind the Marine motto "no better friend, no worse enemy."

It likes the things it knows and doesn't like the things it doesn't. It's the part of us that asserts, takes ownership, fights, stands up, stands for, and defends. It's the "Don't tread on me" flag of the American Revolution and the challenge of the Spartan 300 at Thermopylae when they were invited to surrender their weapons: "Come and get 'em." It's why two-year-olds can treat a stolen toy as if it's the end of the world. *Thumos* marks territory, defends turf, growls at strangers, and defies its leash. It's the pit bull of the soul.

Thumos was the drive I felt inside me to compete and win, what drove Caesar to say that he'd rather be the first of barbarians than the second man in Rome. It was why he wept that by 30 years old he'd done so little compared to Alexander the Great. It was why Alexander wept that his father had left him an orderly kingdom with no chaos to conquer. From Coriolanus to Don Corleone, it's been celebrated and wondered at on stages in a hundred languages. *Thumos* brought Muhammad Ali into the ring and Michael Jordan onto the court. It's ambition incarnate.

Thumos gives reasonable people plenty to roll their eyes at. Left unshaped, it can be like the dog who barks every time a car drives by. It seeks disorder and chaos, so as to step in to be the hero. It creates mountains out of molehills, in order to climb to the top and plant a flag. It treats even a slight offense as a capital one. It's why so many high schoolers end up in the principal's office after a fight over disrespect.

Thumos is inherently interested in worth. It seeks to be superior and dominant and wants to be recognized as such. It competes in everything. When it wins, it gloats; when it loses, it sulks. *Thumos* isn't the kind of guest you'd invite to a cocktail party, but it's your best ally in a bar fight. Despite its uncouth roots, *thumos* is also how America put a man on the moon, an essential part of what drove Crick and Watson to discover the DNA double helix, and the central theme of every Medal of Honor citation.

Most people aren't quite sure what to do with *thumos*. It usually shows up as anger and aggression, as some form of self-assertiveness. It gets people to march and chant, to hold up signs in protest; it leads rival gangs into lethal battles over territory. These days it's more often medicated than shaped or made into something constructive.

But in Sparta, Athens, and all the city-states of Ancient Greece, directing and shaping the power of *thumos* was regarded as essential to the flourishing of both communities and individuals. In its lowest form, it was a hedgehog's defense, prioritizing the preservation of one's own above all else. But when shaped by reason, judgment, and experience, it could become something enterprising too. As the Greeks saw it, *thumos* could, with the right education, become princely.

The Greeks viewed anger as we do a shotgun: In the hands of a criminal, it's terrifying; in the hands of a sheriff, it can be a godsend. It's not my intent here to weigh in on a gun debate but to say that if all the bad people have guns and the good people don't, it's going to be a good day for thieves, drug dealers, and human traffickers. Anger is the same.

In coming to understand *thumos*, I began to appreciate Socrates's image and why anger wouldn't be another hydra head, but was better represented by a lion. The anger that Socrates represented as a lion certainly had the potential to become something ugly when it was paired with an appetite: Some of my peers in high school used to scream and threaten the lunch lady for not giving them big enough portions.

If we let our anger rule, we are consumed by vengeance and victory. We'll become violent with anyone who looks at us the wrong way. We'll sacrifice everything we have for recognition and respect. Prisons are filled with men who let their anger rule over their appetites and minds.

Flourishing, for Socrates, came from the different parts of our souls working together in the right way. When anger could work with the mind, it could create beautiful things, but all three parts needed to be friends with each other. A flourishing soul relied on civilizing the appetites and partnering our anger with our intelligence.

I saw immediate sense in the metaphor, and wanted to get to work ordering my own soul. But as I'd find, getting the parts to work together was a lot tougher than it sounded.

Chapter 2

SMART GUYS FINISH LAST

NEANDERTHAL LOGIC

Critics make good points, but not good movies. This was a key point I was missing when I joined the Marines.

At OCS, the skills that helped me in college were about as useful as knowing how to juggle. I'd gotten used to how teachers talked and how they wanted me to talk. The drill instructors were speaking a different language. I was once ordered to get in line when I was the only person in sight—to get in line with myself! I just stood there. To this day, I have no idea what the right response was.

As I read the written tests, I was constantly confused. "The maximum effective range of the M240 stops at what distance when it's measured?" What does it mean for a max effective range to stop? Did it matter that it was being measured? My peers looked at me like the dumb kid in class. Candidate Koch, a high school quarterback from Oklahoma who'd quickly become my best friend, translated the foreign language for me.

"Max effective range of a 240?" Koch repeated, as if I'd asked what letter came after A. "800 meters."

"Yeah, but they asked what distance the max effective range stopped at when it's measured," I replied, making my case. "And isn't 1,200 meters the max effective range if you put it on a tripod?"

"Stopped at?" Koch was the confused one now. "Max effective range of 240: 800. Who the heck's talking about a tripod?"

"But if it can shoot farther on a tripod than it can without one," I protested, "isn't *that* the maximum range the gun can reach?"

Koch shook his head. "LeBlanc, you've got to be the dumbest smart guy I know."

I was right about the syntax, but got the question wrong. I was at serious risk of being dropped from the Marines for academics! I didn't go to OCS to be sent home as the guy with a story about how the Marines were too stupid to let him in. I could be right or I could get what I wanted. Not both. I had to rethink what OCS wanted from me.

Anywhere on the military base while OCS was in session, there was a good chance you'd hear a drill instructor screaming, "Make a decision, Candidate!" After injuries and physical failures, the next most common cause of being dropped at OCS was not being able to make decisions. They didn't care if you decided to march your platoon off a cliff, just so long as you made the decision quickly and didn't waver.

Getting to an answer was the priority; accuracy was a distant second. But not overthinking anything, avoiding "paralysis by analysis," ran radically counter to my previously successful strategies. I'd done well in school because I'd thought through things carefully. Classmates who breezed through the questions got B's and C's; those who were prepared to measure twice and cut once got A's. The corporate world I'd been bred for wanted me to be detail-oriented.

Marine leaders didn't have time to cross every *t* and dot every *i*. They needed leaders who could cut out everything nonessential, masters of triage and trade-offs. They were teaching me this lesson everywhere, even by giving me a test that was meant to be skimmed. In a battle, I needed to know that when I saw an enemy a kilometer away, my machine gun wouldn't reach them. The rest didn't matter.

This was a critical lesson in getting my anger, the lion, and mind, the small man, to work well together. The mind, too, could be a sort of tyrant, insisting on unimportant facts against all common sense. The mind is too often the kid with his hand raised to correct the teacher when she says that birds can fly. "What about penguins?" he says proudly.

Just as I'd had to learn that compromise and agreement weren't useful in every situation, I had to leave behind my habit of understanding every detail. To succeed as a leader,

I needed what I thought of as Neanderthal Logic, a new way of making sense of the essential things, even when it contradicted the fine print. Neanderthal Logic cuts to the heart of things. It's not interested in edge cases or rare exceptions.

Years later, in one of my classes at Harvard, I worked with some consultants on a project for Boston Children's Hospital to see how they could improve efficiency. It took many days and late nights to create all the fancy charts and graphs in our presentation. But at the end, it seemed to me that our only recommendation was that they should buy a coffee machine.

"Maybe we could offer what the military calls a BLUF?" I suggested to solve the issue. "It's a slide at the beginning that tells the Bottom Line Up Front. Then we can support that with the data." The consultants discarded the idea, telling me the military had no place in what we were doing. But as they moved on, my friend leaned over to me and whispered the reason I was ignored. "We don't have a BLUF because we're bluffing." They didn't have any meaningful insights and they knew it.

Neanderthal Logic begins when *thumos* is disgusted by the smarmy mind. It's the part of you that keeps the giddy brain in check. In the Marines, it's the default. Anyone who tries to use their attorney-mind is quickly crushed with rolled eyes. Politics and business are filled with people who look down on Neanderthal Logic, but those at the top tend to use it all the time. Analysts and congressmen love to argue why things are impossible; business owners and governors love to do the impossible.

PRINCE WITHOUT *THUMOS*

From the outset, Hamlet is at war with himself. He's caught between what ancient philosophy says virtue is and what Christianity asserts. As a Christian, he desperately wants to turn the other cheek; but as a son, he wants bloody revenge on the man who killed his father. Hamlet's worldly ambition, outrage, vengefulness, resentment, and pride all torture him as he tries to put together pieces of disparate worlds that don't quite fit.

Hamlet's challenge is to reconcile his high spiritual ideals with the base world around him, to connect heaven and earth. He wants transcendence but is pulled back to ground by the primal connections with his family. Much as he tries to rise above his awful circumstances, he can't stop thinking about his father's murder and his mother's speedy remarriage.

At 30 years old—the age at which Alexander had conquered most of the known world—Hamlet is still studying philosophy and religion. He's the perpetual grad student who can't find a job that seems worthy of his virtues. Now he's supposed to start slaying enemies? The prince who was dedicated to high-minded cosmopolitanism and rationality is thrust into a barbaric revenge play. His first response is to think himself above it all.

His father didn't have that problem. He was from another, older world. When called upon to defend his country with his life, he did so like a lion, facing the invading king in single combat, a Western showdown for royalty. No cunning tricks; no night-time stealth; no Trojan horses. Just two kings standing for their respective armies or causes, winner take all. But even trials by combat can't avoid the question of what might really be worth dying for.

Honor and beauty often look like silly reasons for doing something. Later, when I started my first robotics company, an employee once threatened a lawsuit over a completely false and easily disproven claim. Our company leadership hardly talked about whether we were in the right. It was an economic decision. Was it more expensive to incur a lawsuit or to settle?

Promises made to people on deathbeds and at funerals are often not kept. Without any trappings of ceremony, such as a last will and testament, time quickly makes dying wishes seem unrealistic and unnecessary. Otherwise attainable dreams for exploring the world and finding your place in it get forever delayed because you can't take time off work. Many couples don't have children simply because there never seems to be a good time.

Smart people like Hamlet are especially prone to letting logistics and economics talk them out of their adventures. Those with the highest IQs are often the people who can most quickly tell you why doing something for beauty or honor's sake is a bad idea. Triumph looks childish; principle looks stubborn and unreasonable. Wanting to die when your love leaves you is for the naive; there are plenty of fish in the sea. Risking your life in war or battle is a foolish miscalculation; nothing like that's worth dying for.

What Hamlet is missing, what the Marines were looking for, and the reason why past a certain point happiness statistics don't correlate with intelligence, all point to the same sort of problem: *Thumos* isn't as stuck up as intelligence to think that it's above the particular things around it. When suitably shaped, it's ready to take on the beautiful irrationalities of loyalty, courage, duty, and devotion. Properly aligned, it seeks victory over small-minded monetary concerns and scoffs at material considerations. It stands for principle, honor, dominance, superiority, distinction, and recognition. As Napoleon famously wondered, "It's amazing what a man will do for a piece of colored ribbon." Left unchecked, *thumos* easily falls into the destructive and criminal. Hamlet, a heavenly prince condemned to earth, fails to tame and civilize the warrior beast inside himself. Tragedy is inevitable.

VICTIMS OF EQUALITY

The Marine Corps was my first experience of a place where inequalities were treated seriously. In my 18 years of schooling before OCS, I hadn't much appreciated how a misty veil of equality had been draped over nearly everything else. No one was inferior. More importantly, no one was superior. We were all supposed to be equal.

The Marine Corps nonchalantly tore off that veil, burned it, and never said a word about it. They didn't care about race, age, or where you were from. Those differences seemed to disappear when everyone's head was shaved and we all had to shuffle naked through the showers. But in the Marine Corps, no one pretended that we were all equal in value. Some Marines were good; some weren't.

Good in the Marine Corps boiled down to 14 leadership traits, among which were courage, loyalty, and judgment.

Nor were those leadership traits simply hung on the wall and recited by recruits either. They were the formal categories by which all Marine leaders were judged and ranked at regular intervals throughout their careers. Good in the Marine Corps was doing 20 dead-hang pull-ups. Twelve was bad.

The reason is simple. War, for all its ambiguity and gray areas, is unapologetic about its end: victory. The Marine Corps wasn't about making sure that weak people were treated fairly. War and the requirements of victory didn't treat them fairly. The Marine Corps was about creating strong, clever killers. Even so, some candidates insisted on fairness.

Adams was making his third attempt at OCS. In the civilian world he was a lawyer, used to arguing a case and getting his way. One day he came in nearly last place on an endurance course, a six-mile run through the woods and swamps of Quantico, navigating obstacles with a 30-pound pack.

He wasn't going to get dropped again, so Adams made his case: He insisted he'd been issued a bad pack. One of the weight-bearing straps was broken and he carried it around with him as evidence, as he pleaded his case to anyone who'd listen. But no one listened. Nobody cared.

His case relied on a sense of fairness. The strap was broken; other Marines had been issued better straps. It wasn't as if Adams could stop by the store to get a new one; it had broken during the event. It wasn't fair. Adams had been put at a disadvantage by something out of his control. He wanted a do-over or at least to be exempted from the shame of losing.

In law school, where Adams had spent many years, those

would have been strong arguments. But this wasn't that kind of school. The Marines had an answer for faulty gear: "Adapt and overcome." What Adams didn't understand was that every candidate could find reasons for what might have prevented them from finishing fast. Some had light injuries that they pushed through to stay in the course. Many, in the Virginia winter, were sick. And a good number of them had faulty gear, since this was OCS and not the front lines. Most of the issue looked like it was from Vietnam.

Adams was later dropped. I could imagine him back in some college town telling the story of his broken pack to anyone who'd listen. In the civilian world, people listened to stories like that. They'd respond, "Well, that's not fair," with a tone of indignation. The Marine Corps would become the idiot in Adams's story, the fools who dropped a great candidate for something beyond his control.

In the Marines, leaders needed more than evidence and excuses, even if they were good ones. Marine culture had long ago decided that regardless of how successful Adams's tactics might be in the civilian world, they weren't the traits that won wars. As I watched him pack up his things, I started to question the arguments and excuses my own mind was making. They wouldn't do me any good here.

UGLY ROOTS

In high school, I thought of my emotions as my true self. Back then I was told to do what I love, to be true to myself, and to do what makes me happy. If my teachers knew even the slightest bit about my passions as a teenager, I have no doubt they would've stopped encouraging me to follow them. Still, I believed in my appetites as the authentic me.

In college, I loved the idea of being rational, which made me want to rid myself of emotions completely. I'd often be so immersed in a book that I would only stop reading when I suddenly realized I was shivering, my stomach was growling, and I had to sprint to the bathroom. I resented my appetites. Outside of them, I felt so sophisticated. I even wore a cardigan.

By the time I was becoming a Marine, I'd started resenting my mind. I was so sick of hearing arguments without action. I couldn't stand to hear people analyzing the same plans and worrying about the same risks. I didn't want to think; I didn't want to feel; I wanted to *do*. When I told my parents I was joining the Marines, I dismissed my mom's tears as too emotional and my dad's arguments as too safe. I was going to the action.

Shutting down my mind and appetites in practice, though, made me go back to a weird passage in Homer's *Odyssey*, which is a weird book to begin with. Not many readers remember the small detail where Hermes shows Odysseus the moly plant, but OCS finally made some sense of that passage to me. The image of the plant became a sort of North Star for me as I navigated the rest of my training.

Odysseus faces great challenges as he and his crew try to sail back home from the Trojan War. One of their adventures finds them on the island of Circe, an enchantress. When Odysseus sends half his crew to investigate some signs of habitation, they encounter the witch and she turns them into pigs.

Odysseus goes to save his men, but receives some advice first from Hermes, the messenger of the gods.

To make Odysseus immune to Circe's powers, Hermes shows him the moly plant, which has a milk-white flower and black roots. Strangely enough, Odysseus doesn't need to ingest the moly to gain immunity; simply seeing it pulled from the ground is enough to protect him from being turned into a pig.

In the moly, the dark roots are connected to the pure flower. They're a unified whole. Odysseus was led to perceive a connection between the primal wants that got his men turned into pigs and the more beautiful, developed conduct that might bring them safely home. Likewise, noble ambition can grow from selfish and greedy roots; sexual instinct can become the glue of successful marriage and the source of a flourishing family; protection of one's seed can grow into a father's love for his son. Virtue, like the beautiful moly, relies on its darker roots in order to exist above the ground, in one's conduct. Instinct and appetite can't be tyrannically suppressed. They must be given their due.

This is why I hesitate every time I hear parents want to eradicate bullying, or when I hear people talk about getting rid of their pride. Can bullying be bad? Absolutely. But if its roots aren't somehow integral to who human beings are, why is it reported behavior in every culture and time period? Envy can be ugly and small, but it can also motivate us to expand who we are. Gossip can trash people's reputations, but it also keeps a check on bad yet legal behavior and helps us know who we might need to avoid.

In the moly plant, Odysseus faced and understood a deep

truth about the human soul: that our godlike minds must live in unity and integrity with our bodily drives.

IT'S GOD'S FAULT

My mind was good at telling me why I wasn't to blame. For anything that went wrong, I had quick excuses, no problems listing what other factors might have played into the failure. The bodily fact, for example, may have been that I'd run 3 miles in 20 minutes when I was supposed to finish in 18. But my mind would argue that my legs were tired from a run the day before. OCS helped train me to fend off the mind and its selfish calculations in such debates. It taught me to start owning the facts on the ground.

In one such lesson, my OCS platoon had failed to complete a scheduled 10-mile hike after we'd been hit by a surprise snowstorm. We had no say in the events of our training. The sergeant instructors—essentially drill instructors for OCS—had canceled the hike due to safety concerns. Still, that didn't stop Gunnery Sergeant Gomez from using our unanticipated downtime to teach us a lesson.

He called the platoon to attention and paced down the aisle between us, disgusted. I stared straight ahead like I'd been caught in the woods by a grizzly. No sudden movements. No eye contact.

Another candidate, freshly out of college and, like most of us, wearing a uniform for the first time, wasn't so lucky. Gomez moved in on him like a shark at the smell of blood.

"Why you fail to complete the hike?" he said in a thick accent.

"This candidate," he began—Marine candidates aren't allowed to say the word *I*—"did not complete the hike because the sergeant instructors canceled it, Gunnery Sergeant!"

"But I'm a sergeant instructor," Gomez said dramatically, casting himself as the accused but innocent victim. "It's my fault you failed to complete the hike?"

"No, Gunnery Sergeant!" the candidate recovered. "The sergeant instructor cadre canceled the hike, Gunnery Sergeant!"

"But I'm a Sergeant Instructor Gunnery, am I not?!" Gomez screamed.

"Yes, Gunnery Sergeant Gomez!" the candidate yelled.

"The sergeant instructor cadre wants you to be conditioned, Candidate," Gunnery Sergeant Gomez screamed back. "Why would they cancel a conditioning hike?!"

"The snowstorm made the hike unsafe, Gunnery Sergeant Gomez! The instructor cadre cares about safety!" the candidate yelled, hoping to score some flattery points.

"They canceled because it snowed," Gomez clarified. "And why did it snow, Candidate?!"

The candidate didn't know how to respond. But at OCS, a wrong answer fast was better than a right answer slow. "Barometric pressures, Gunnery Sergeant Gomez!" he tried.

"Bare-metric pressures?!" The drill instructor looked as though he would lose his mind. "Bare-metric preeeeessuuuuuures?!"

"The weather, Gunnery Sergeant!" the candidate shouted, hoping to get back into safer waters.

"It was the weather's fault!" Gomez screamed as though unhinged. He got within an inch of the candidate's face. "And who controls the weather?!"

"God! Gunnery Sergeant Gomez!" the candidate screamed in a final plea.

He released his focus on the platoon commander and directed his rage toward all of us. "You all think you can be Marine officers! Marine officers don't blame barometric pressure! Marine officers take accountability! Disgusting candidates think it's Gunnery Sergeant Gomez's fault! It's the weather's fault! It's *God's* fault! The disgusting candidates failed to complete their hike! Sergeant instructors don't need to hike. Weather doesn't need to hike. *God* didn't fail to complete His 10-mile conditioning hike. But it's everyone else's fault, right?" He slammed the door to his office, leaving us in silence.

Many wrote the scene off as what Marines call a "fuck-fuck game," a psychological test designed to weed out psychologically weak candidates. But I took something more from it. There were always reasons to account for failure, things out of your control. Analytically, it was easy to put the blame on those reasons. But in the world of competition, victory doesn't care why you fell short. The gold medal doesn't come with an asterisk. Neither do bullets.

My mind was a practiced defense lawyer, always coming up with ways to suggest reasonable doubt when I would be blamed. It was prudent and risk averse. My mind wanted down-side protection and loved to find evidence for why my loss was someone else's fault. The analytic mind is always preparing to lose—it doesn't want to be blamed for being rash. But in doing so, it loses all ability for daring and bold actions. It won't take a shot for fear of shooting itself in the foot.

It reminds me of one of the first marketing campaigns I ever designed. My first company made robots that replaced security guards. Skeptical customers would always say the same thing: Robots can't do what our guards do. So I played on that theme by showing our robots doing all the bad things guards did. I had a photo of our robot looking at its phone instead of patrolling. I showed the robot watching TV, asleep at its desk, and drinking from a flask.

Security buyers thought it was hilarious. But my marketing company, who I paid a lot of money to, talked me out of it, laughing at my naivete. It risked being offensive to customers and ruining our reputation. We went with bland ads instead. They didn't get us any business but looked like a responsible marketing spend.

My idea might have been the talk of the conference, something that got customers to really think about why they'd replace guards. But if it hadn't worked, if it did offend customers, I would have been ridiculed. I can hear the people around me now: "How could you have thought that calling security guards alcoholics would get them to like you?" I wouldn't have had a good defense.

Thumos wins because it's bold. The lion doesn't care how it caught the gazelle so long as it's eating. *Thumos* didn't need to explain its win. Later, critics love to say why winners got lucky, why their fundamentals were unsound, why they should have lost. Fittingly, *thumos* doesn't pay much attention to critics.

If you're explaining, you're losing. "Scoreboard," as my dad would always say when I was busy rationalizing a loss—meaning that the finest commentary in the world can't change the score at the end of the game. When you were playing to win, it didn't matter why you lost. You cared what number was next to your name.

GAMING THE GAME

Integrity had always seemed clean and easy growing up. But after joining the Marine Corps, I had to learn the balance between doing what's right and getting things done. It's not hard to find a Marine who left something out of his medical history to get into the military. Bureaucracies don't care much for nuance. But in basketball, there's a difference between throwing an elbow and pulling a knife. I was having a hard time navigating that line in my training.

I'd joined the Marines thinking that every Marine was in the infantry, fighting on the front lines. It turned out there were 21 other jobs, many of which would never see combat. The Basic School (TBS) was a six-month course that determined who would fight in the infantry and who would process travel claims. If I got a noncombat job, my dreams would be shattered.

Choosing the jobs followed a funny process where finishing higher in the rankings didn't automatically equate with a higher pick. By the odd rules they used, I would have a very late pick if I aced the test, but one of the first choices if I bombed it.

I couldn't decide what to do. *Thumos* didn't like things like this. There were plenty of my peers content to take the test to the best of their ability and let the chips fall where they may. But my mind was now arguing a thumotic point back to me: Scoreboard. If you joined the Marines and became an aircraft mechanic who never went to war, you were hoping for an asterisk. The mind had a simple, clever plan that could get me on the path to war. I decided to bomb the test.

That afternoon, my name was called along with six others. We were led to an empty classroom. Not too long after, the executive officer (XO) came in—a combat decorated infantry officer whom I'd never seen smile. "You all know why you're here," he said forcefully. Clearly, I wasn't the only one with the bright idea of bombing the test. He was pissed. We were screwed. "Integrity is one of the 14 leadership traits. Without it, none of the others matter."

"This morning," he continued, "the company commander and I have been deciding what to do with you integrity violators. We're considering everything, including having you dishonorably discharged." With that, he walked out.

We sat anxiously in silence for several hours. Finally, another captain came in with a stack of papers. "This," he said, "is yesterday's test. You're going to retake it. If you get over 80%, you'll graduate TBS. If you don't, you'll either retake the entire course or will face more serious charges. Your two hours begin now."

We retook the test, this time honestly, and returned to our platoons. I waited in anticipation for more news, but it never came. I never got my new test score. No one ever followed up with more threats or spoke of dishonorable discharge. Nothing. The next week, when they posted the final class rankings, it was the test I'd bombed that had been counted. I was in the top of the second third. I became the eighth person out of 300 to choose my job.

Part of me thought that what I'd done was simply disgraceful. Yet there was a bit of Neanderthal Logic that took pride in what I'd done as well. Despite playing a dirty trick, I'd come to the Marines to become an infantry officer and I was going to become one. No asterisks, no excuses.

I've told this story to friends outside the Marines who have been appalled at what I did. But whenever I told it to any of my peers from training, no one has ever thought it was a big deal.

It wasn't until years later, running my first company, that I understood the story more clearly. There, I had a lot of employees working all kinds of different projects. There were some who I knew would always come back and tell me why what I'd asked them to do was impossible. There were others who got the job done. They tended to break the rules, but they never broke any laws. Those were the kind of people I wanted on my team.

I'd certainly crossed some lines to become an infantry officer, lines I couldn't have imagined crossing before I joined. But as I was learning to become part of a team, I started to realize that some things that sounded wrong were exactly why people liked having me on their team. Part of *thumos* can accept suffering in prison if you've been caught fair and square in battle. But the mind knows that the right thing to do is to hatch an escape plan right away.

It had taken a clever plot, but I'd satisfied a lionlike desire.

I was going to go to war. There's no shortage of people who believe in a more rigid integrity. They insist that any move like mine is ugly and that it's more beautiful to suffer the consequences.

I always try to think about how I might look at my own son in these situations. If he'd broken into the instructor's drawer and stolen the test, that would clearly be ugly. But failing on purpose looked clever and almost fair. After all, was it reasonable for the Marine Corps to ask me to act against my own self-interest? To get me to study for a test to my own detriment? If I were watching my son, I'd rather see him do what he joined the Marines to do.

"Me Against the World" is an embarrassing yet necessary phase in understanding *thumos*, anger, resentment, bitterness, aggression, and assertiveness. To understand what a lever does, one way is to pull it hard and watch what happens. When *thumos* is engaged in full, it manifests as an assertive independence. It's looking for a fight. To understand how we'll use our anger, we first have to let our anger free; we need to open ourselves to the risks of challenging and disagreeing with almost anything.

As I took on the rest of the world, I started to understand more about Socrates's image of the soul. It was clear now why anger is a lion. Anger is powerful and dangerous, yet it can be used toward beautiful ends. The hydra can clearly be a monster, but life is better when it's fed moderately, rather than starved. It was also clear that the small man, the analytic mind, although he should be in charge, shouldn't be given free rein either. Without the lion or the hydra insisting on their own claims, the small man can be tyrannical, calculating, and dull.

Before I came across Socrates's strange metaphor in Plato's *Republic*, I'd thought of the soul in terms of mind and body. I was attracted to the power of mind over matter, of romanticizing what it would be like to have my mind make all my decisions, ignoring all emotions and pleasures. Plato, through Socrates, however, added a third part for me to think about. Suddenly it felt as though I'd nearly discarded an entire third of my soul!

To become the man I wanted to be, *thumos*, anger, and aggression needed to be understood and dealt with fairly. Each part alone was inadequate to rule, but as a properly coordinated group, I was starting to see how they might make a life. The congress of appetites, aggression, and mind was a committee that could work. Compromise from the get-go wasn't the right starting point for what I was exploring, but its role in the story clearly wasn't over.

Flexing my insistence on independence showed me something else too: I wasn't a solo act. Becoming the best wasn't something I could do alone. Even more, it was obvious that I naturally wanted friends. Koch, Kimball, and Lewis—they're in my life by mere accident of the alphabet—had all become my friends. I defended them. I joked with them. I cared what happened to them. The militant robot I'd hoped to be, the one without friends and without pleasures, wasn't who I wanted to become.

Through the process of starting to get my soul in order,

it seemed I'd graduated to a new stage: Us v. Them. Now, it was my team versus the world. But even that new framing didn't keep my mind from straying into Machiavellian territory, into becoming a bit too calculating. It would take a lot more for me to understand how to get along with my growing team.

PART I
RETROSPECTIVE

- Shame and embarrassment can be powerful tools in shaping yourself (see "Not a War Story," page 3).
- The mind should direct anger and appetites, but like political constituents. There are negotiations, backroom deals, and compromises no one likes. Anger and appetites deserve a say (see "Anger, Obviously, Isn't the Answer," page 6).
  - *Appetites*
    - You might think you'll be happiest by giving wholly in to your pleasures (sex, food, drugs, etc.), but you run the risk of becoming a slave to your appetites ("Anger, Obviously, Isn't the Answer," page 6; "The Lion Emerges," page 15).
    - You might think you'll be better off denying your

appetites, but food isn't just fuel, sex isn't just sensation, and alcohol isn't just an escape (see "Comfort-Based Decisions," page 12; "Ugly Roots," page 31; "Machine Guns Up," page 56).
    - The best way to deal with appetites is to find the moderate space between indulgence and denial. It's best to govern them with habits, allowing them to give your life color and substance, pleasure and satisfaction.
  - *Anger*
    - Distinguish between tantrums and convictions of honor. Squash the former, act on the latter.
    - Don't get angry at things that are ordinary or unavoidable.
    - High-mindedness can lure people into feeling that they're above fights they should be engaged in; righteous anger protects the things it loves when they're attacked (see "Too Smart for Anger," page 14).
- You may resent that you've been cast in a particular role, but it's still yours to play (see "Prince Without *Thumos*," page 27).
- Anger and aggression have their opinions but they themselves don't belong simply to the mind. And while they may seem irrational, they're not simply feelings either. They don't fit neatly into the logic-emotion, thinking-feeling, or mind-body splits we often talk about. The Greeks saw them as a third part of us, and one that needs a different sort of education (see "The Wisdom of Athens," page 19).
- It's easy to get overly proud of yourself for knowing details

and specifics. But there's an art to cutting through details to get to the heart of things (see "Neanderthal Logic," page 23).

- The mind tends to think happiness is nothing but success. Smart people often overlook how rich, full lives are usually more about family, friends, and well-formed pleasures.
- You don't get extra credit for struggling. There are two main strategies for getting people to think you've achieved something: (1) achieve more, or (2) tell them how hard it was to achieve what you already have. Many people try to enlarge their lives by telling a story of how hard the struggle was. It's better to build by downplaying struggle and achieving more (see "The Lion Emerges," page 15).
- You don't need to eradicate envy, pride, gossip, bullying, assertiveness, anger, resentment, sulking, and greed. They need to be shaped. The captain of industry has harnessed his greed; the Medal of Honor winner has focused his anger (see "Ugly Roots," page 31).
- The mind naturally formulates good reasons for why it lost. That tendency keeps you from doing bold things. But you often win doing something inexplicably bold and seemingly rash (see "It's God's Fault," page 34; "Victims of Equality," page 29).
- The mind tends to detach from particular things, but the best life demands standing up for and sometimes even dying for what you love (see "Prince Without *Thumos*," page 27).
- There's a difference between drifting over the line and crashing through the guardrail. Integrity doesn't mean rigidity (see "Gaming the Game," page 38).

Part II

FRIENDS, ENEMIES, AND STRANGERS

Chapter 3

YOU WANT ME TO WIN WITH THESE PEOPLE?

CHIMPANZEE POLITICS

Teams love a winner, but they hate a star. Whatever critiques I'd later have of myself as a young Marine, I worked hard to be the best. To me, that should've been enough for every team to want to have me. I came to resent anyone who questioned my way of doing things. I thought that winning should be enough to earn me the top slot on the team. In life, though, that's rarely the case.

Frans de Waal's *Chimpanzee Politics* was one of the best account's I'd come across of dominance hierarchy and teams. The story focuses on three chimps—Luit, Yeroen, and Nikki—who vie constantly with one another over becoming the alpha in a band of some 30 apes at the Arnhem Zoo in the Netherlands. Over the seven years they were observed, each had his time on top, though none ever ruled uncontested. Marine training told a similar story.

Prestige battles were constant, just like those apes fighting over who'd be the alpha. My clash with Kincaid was particularly bad. He was a politician. Early and shamelessly, he sucked up to the priors—lieutenants who'd previously been enlisted. He'd gain their favor by talking trash about how the other new guys didn't belong in the Marine Corps. He'd go after me personally, belittling my experience compared with theirs. The priors liked that.

One day during a bayonet exercise—in which Marines led four-man teams through a course in the woods, stabbing the dummies that were hung from trees as they went—Kincaid looked at me and smirked. We were natural rivals in this sort of thing.

Kincaid's team left first, then another, and then mine. The Marines on my team happened to be not very fast and I bolted out in front. When I reached the first three dummies—which we were supposed to attack together—I stabbed each in quick succession, spilling the red-colored corn starch that was designed to look like blood. Then I sprinted forward.

An instructor caught up with me and yelled, "You're only as fast as your slowest Marine!" I turned around and sprinted back to my team yelling, "Let's go! Let's go!" Grudgingly, they sped up. We passed the team in front of us and got eyes on Kincaid's. His voice was raised, but he was being much more diplomatic: nicer, though less effective. I kept yelling at my team to keep up, stabbing all the dummies myself. We passed Kincaid's team and crossed the finish line.

Later that day, Kincaid approached me with an apparently friendly tone. I figured he was there to extend an olive branch and I was ready to accept. I hated the thought of being locked in a childish antagonism and was eager to clear the air. After a few niceties, he said, "Can I give you some advice?"

There was the Kincaid I knew. He was getting ready to beat me over the head with his olive branch and I'd be damned if I was going to let him. "Why the fuck would I listen to your advice?" I asked, suddenly sharp.

"Don't be like that," he said, still pretending to be a peacekeeper. "I just wanted to say you shouldn't try so hard to beat everyone all the time. You're going to need friends someday and you aren't making any."

"I see," I sarcastically replied. "So you lose at everything to make friends. Smart."

"Just trying to help, LeBlanc," Kincaid said, shaking his head like a dad whose advice just couldn't break through.

The exchange infuriated me. He'd tried to get under my skin and it had worked. Even worse, as much as I hated to admit it, he had a point. My team had resented me for pushing them. Although Kincaid's team lost, they were all pals, sharing jokes about the fake blood. I felt a bit embarrassed for going so hard, as though I'd won a three-legged race at a family reunion by dragging my cousin's toddler on my leg.

In *Chimpanzee Politics*, the alpha isn't decided merely by the physical battles, though they do play a crucial role.

Challengers would help the females take care of babies and would share food with the others. While Luit, Yeroen, and Nikki all took their turns on top, they only ever gained power through coalition and cooperation.

Among the chimpanzees, the alpha was most consistently measured by how often the other apes would greet him with an upturned hand, a gesture of respect. I was winning the contests, but Kincaid was the one getting high fives. He was a part of the brotherhood. I was not. When I'd first planned for the Marines, I'd imagined that honor was won through contest. But I was now seeing that the challenge was richer and more complex than that.

Condescending as it was for Kincaid, my peer, to offer me advice after he lost, I'd been no less arrogant. I hadn't found it easy to fraternize with the other lieutenants. Apart from a few of them, I treated most of my platoon as faceless competition. I resented them for not recognizing my potential, and they resented me for not respecting their accomplishments and skills. If I really wanted to be number one, domination wouldn't work. The top Marines were held up by willing Marines beneath them. I was a long way from trusting anyone not to drop me.

MOSES'S PEOPLE

The hard lessons I was learning echoed the classics I'd studied. I read the Great Books in college, everything from Homer's *Iliad* to Einstein on relativity. When I first looked over the reading list when I was applying, I was surprised to see the Bible on the curriculum. As part of a full education, it was meant to be read and studied just like any of the other classics. Although I hadn't opened it since Sunday school, I felt confident that I couldn't learn anything more from the simplistic stories I remembered. As I became a Marine, however, I saw some of those stories through a new lens.

When I was a kid, Moses had looked to me like another boring old man with a beard, a simple conduit for God's power. Later, in my 20s and filled with ambition, I started to appreciate just how difficult his undertaking really was. Nothing about Moses's story seemed simple to me anymore. He looked instead like one of the princes I was fascinated with, no less a leader than was Caesar, Henry V, or Abraham Lincoln.

As Moses leads his people through a 40-year trek in the desert, they drag their feet, whine, and regularly forget where they're going. It takes nearly half of Exodus before we learn even one of the names of the people he leads. It's not clear that Moses cares to learn any of those names. The Hebrew people figure as little more than the unbalanced load he's been charged with carrying to freedom.

But as he grows into his role as a leader, Moses learns to take ownership not just of all their hardships but of his people as well. On their way to the Promised Land, the people break from God, deciding instead to worship a golden calf. This isn't the first time they've disobeyed Moses or God. They've regularly resisted spiritual commands in favor of their own mundane and material wants. Although it's important for the people to learn once again that they must seek something higher than this world, the incident is pivotal in Moses's own journey.

God, acting as though the golden calf is a sort of last straw, offers Moses the option of ditching the Hebrew people altogether. He'll give Moses a new people, his own people, that he can take to the Promised Land. It's the first time God has made such an offer. But Moses, who has resented the people throughout, finds in this moment that he has developed an attachment to them. He turns down God's offer, protecting those he'd been appointed to lead. When Moses later recounts the story, his telling is the first time he uses "we" instead of "I." It was in that act that they went from God's people to his people.

In my own case, becoming a leader was initially about distinguishing myself. I wanted to finish first; I wanted to be better. But as I thought back to Moses, I realized that my spiritual journey toward becoming a good leader had just begun. Command without care for the commanded is tyranny. True command came from a sort of trust, even a kind of love. I was competing to earn the title of Marine officer, but I still felt like an outsider. I was being taught to lead my peers, yet I was failing to win their trust. I was failing to make them my own. I had to learn how to build trust.

MACHINE GUNS UP

The Infantry Officer Course (IOC) was the first time I was part of a team that I wanted to win for. All Marine lieutenants had gone to TBS. But IOC had to be earned. "In 10 weeks," an instructor had told us on the first day, "this will be the most lethal company in the world. Nowhere else will every member of a company know how to call for artillery, how to call for an air strike, how to fire a TOW missile. Nowhere else will they all be proficient in land navigation and leading troops in battle."

I'd always looked at the other Marines as my competition. At IOC, I saw them as my true peers. It was the first place I realized that there were other Marines of my rank who I looked up to. I didn't want to let them down.

I was in a dead sprint, straight up the side of a mountain, trying to crouch with ammo strapped across my chest and ammo cans in both of my hands. Infantry training had moved from the forest winter to the desert heat. I was the machine gun team leader and my graduation from IOC depended on this performance.

In the exercise, my dozen Marines and I were tasked with setting up a machine gun position on top of a mountain, shooting at the enemy head-on, while 40 Marines on the ground attacked. It was support by fire, a textbook tactical maneuver. Our rounds would divert the enemy's defense and fix them in place, allowing the attacking unit to get close and destroy their flank.

But to get to our position, my team had to carry hundreds of pounds in ammo and weapons up a mountain. As soon as the enemy saw us (in this exercise, when the instructors yelled "machine guns up!"), we needed to get to our positions as fast as possible and start firing. In every attempt, we were spotted just at the foot of the mountain, meaning we had to sprint up a steep hill to our positions, only to find that our Marines on the ground had already been killed.

We'd run the course four times, exhausted and failing

each run. After suffering with these Marines for two months, I didn't feel distant from them anymore. I was ashamed to let them down. I badly wanted to give them a chance to win. Yet from what I could tell, the instructors had the exercise rigged. It was TBS all over again, but I wasn't going to let my Marines get cheated.

I went to the instructor and complained that he was calling "machine guns up" too early. I accused him of fixing the game so that we'd lose. I told him I didn't care whether he marked me as a bad commander and dropped me from the course. I wanted him to give my Marines a fair shot.

The instructor heard me out without getting angry or marking me as a weak leader. Once I'd finished, he told me exactly how the exercise worked. Instructors were placed with the enemy and called him on his radio when they saw us. The exercise didn't begin until the enemy was actually able to see us. It was completely fair.

With that information, I had an idea. The instructors had given us the route we'd been sprinting: straight up the mountain to our gun positions. But what if we didn't go that route? We'd accepted it as a test of grit, but did it have to be? I thought I might have another way to win.

On the next iteration, I instructed the team that we wouldn't run. Instead, we crept up the hill slowly on a different route, helping each other carry the heavy guns and ammo. This time, we could have done jumping jacks and the enemy wouldn't have seen us. We were on the opposite side of the mountain.

During the previous attempts, we'd tripped and fallen into our gun positions as the instructor yelled. This time, we crawled into them and set up our positions like we were setting the table for dinner. Marines even had time to put their earplugs in. Once my Marines were set, I called over my radio to the Marines on the ground: "Machine guns up."

We opened fire, holding the enemy in their trenches. Our attacking unit moved toward them without sprinting and thus with plenty of energy to attack and destroy them in the trenches. My team was elated.

In the final huddle where instructors gave lessons learned, the lead instructor who'd been watching for machine guns said that this was the best they'd ever seen a class do. In his remarks, he credited the machine gun team, saying this was the first time the team took the positions without being spotted.

I'd tricked my way into IOC when I'd purposely bombed a test to "game the game." In that case, I'd pulled a trick to help myself. At IOC, I'd solidified my slot as an infantry officer by finding a similar trick, but one that benefited my team. It wasn't so ugly when it was in service of the team relying on me.

At the end of the course, we built a massive bonfire, feasted on roasted pig, and drank all night. Preparing for the Marines, I'd given up feasts, parties, and binges, thinking that the ideal Marine didn't give in to those pleasures. But that night I saw that the spirit of celebration was exactly what a band of brothers should be embracing.

Our class elected me to emcee the festivities, where they pushed me to do my impressions of our instructors and roast our peers. I was surprised to find myself so honored when they selected me to do it. They weren't a faceless group of allies holding me up. We were friends, laughing together and sharing stories. That night, I felt such camaraderie that I knew I'd left the idea of Me Against the World behind.

BENEVOLENT TYRANNY

When training was finally over, I received orders to my first command, where I'd see that my team-building would be put to the test. These weren't my peers now; they were my first subordinates. The role had been a bit of a surprise after my training. I'd always thought I'd go directly to Afghanistan. Instead, I was sent to the desert in California. I wasn't leading a platoon of 50 Marines in combat as I'd hoped. Instead, I had six Marines and my job was to manage intelligence for the unit. In California, intelligence mostly consisted of briefing the weather report in meetings. Still, I intended to do well with the first Marines in my command.

Without an officer in charge, the Marines I inherited lacked discipline. I started them on building briefs and presentations, work that tested them and kept them busy. I soon learned exactly how far behind they were.

"Just label Iraq on the map," I told Lance Corporal Dudley, as we built our first brief.

"Yes, sir," Dudley replied. "Which one is Iraq?"

Dudley wasn't alone. Only one of my six analysts was able to identify Iraq on a map of the Middle East. *Here's why I'm in charge*, I thought. I envisioned teaching them not only Iraq's location but the location of every other country in the world. I'd engage them in sophisticated foreign policy discussions. It would be my legacy.

I gathered my Marines and briefed them on their new assignment. "Whenever you find yourself without a task, pull out a map and study the countries of the Middle East. There's a quiz on Friday." Almost immediately, I had the beginnings of a mutiny on my hands. They wanted to know why, lied about being busy, and told me that this wasn't elementary school. "You're right," I replied in the sort of retort I'd made a habit. "An elementary school student could identify Iraq on a map."

They were angry. I was angry. Dudley stood up. "And what if we don't learn? What if we just fail your test?" It was a challenge I had in fact prepared for. Unless everyone passed with at least 80%, we'd all run six miles. I was pleased with the incentives I'd set to get them working as a team. I pictured them quizzing each other late at night, all trying to ace the test to show me that I'd underestimated them.

On the day of the test, only one Marine got over 80%. The others hadn't studied at all. Dudley tried to get 0%, but accidentally got some right.

"OK," I said confidently. "If you're going to be dumb, you'd better be fast. Get changed. We've got six miles to run." I led my analysts on a six-mile run in the desert at a seven-minute pace. One Marine fell out during the first mile; Dudley threw up after about 10 minutes. I slowed the pace. We all completed the run.

The same day next week, I gave the same quiz with the same rules. All but one Marine failed. We ran another six miles. This time, I wore my 30-pound flak jacket to help me set a slower pace, and as we ran, I gave them an impromptu lecture on Iran's ambition for hegemony. Dudley threw up again.

We continued in that pattern over six weeks. After the first two, another gave in and aced the test. After six, I had everyone but Dudley. At week seven, under pressure from his peers, Dudley finally gave in and passed the quiz.

Each week after that, they were required to learn the countries of a new continent. We did this until they could identify at least 80% of the countries in the world. We never had to run again.

I'd gotten control. I'd out-worked and out-studied them. Finally, they bent the knee. But I discovered that there was little satisfaction in getting them to submit. I wasn't a good king; I was just a bad boss. They hated me. No one wanted to work for me. Instead of being a proud group dedicated to excellence, they were ashamed to serve under me. Their friends all knew about the deal and thought I was an idiot for making them run. Yet their friends also thought they were idiots for refusing to learn something they should already know. We were the laughingstock of the battalion.

None of them was ever going to be an expert in geography or foreign policy. They didn't need to be. I could have worked with them better, worked at their pace, and won their affection so that they wanted to follow me. Instead, I'd traded in all my carrots for sticks, and beat them until they ran as fast as I demanded. My tyrannical success was no more satisfying than cutting a puzzle piece with scissors to make it fit.

WINNING THE WRONG GAME

Even before I'd met Dudley and my other Marines, I'd gotten off on the wrong foot with our commanding officer (CO), Lieutenant Colonel Halloway. When I'd checked into the unit, I was learning about my assignment in the office next to the CO. Halloway, overhearing me, yelled, "Is that the Deuce?!" using a reductive nickname for intelligence officers that I didn't much like. "Get him in here!"

I entered his office and stood at attention six inches from the front of his desk, trying hard to remember whether it was supposed to be twelve. "Good morning, sir!" I shouted, in the hope that some enthusiasm might cover up my ignorance of the protocol. "Second Lieutenant LeBlanc reporting."

"Fucking Deuce," he said, sitting back in his chair with what could only be described as a shit-eating grin. His hands were on his head and his gut stuck out proudly. He didn't release me from attention. I wasn't checking in; I was kissing the ring and he was making me beg for it. He picked up my bio from his desk. "You went to IOC?" he asked.

"Yes, sir," I replied, understanding that we were already headed down a bad path.

"Sniper Leaders Course?" he continued, reading the paper in front of him. "Certified instructor of foreign weapons?"

"Yes, sir."

His smile left his face. "You must think you're pretty fucking cool," he said.

"Sir?" I shifted my weight, still standing at attention.

"I said you must think you're pretty fucking cool, Deuce,"

he repeated. "You must think God put you on earth to lead Marines in combat, to deploy to combat zones, to kill Taliban. And instead, you're here with me."

He stared at me and I stared back, wishing there was a way to make it seem less aggressive. We were in some sort of high-stakes poker game and I didn't know how to fold. I wanted to reset our relationship somehow, to apologize for whatever I'd done to make him hate me. But I continued to hold my position and keep eye contact.

Finally, his face morphed back into a sort of drunkard's smile. "Deucey," he said, which suddenly made "Deuce" sound like a reasonable compromise. "We're going to get along great."

My first task in my first billet was to build a great terrain model for Lieutenant Colonel Halloway. Terrain models are usually simple sketches done with a stick in the dirt, aimed at showing the main features, such as mountains and rivers, and helping each Marine to get a sense of where he'd be going. On this occasion, though, Halloway saw the model as an opportunity for us to do something special. He told me his vision for the model and I took notes, ready to execute.

With the shovels, yarn, twine, and laminated note cards I'd bought at a local store, I used up the few precious drops of my fledgling authority driving my Marines to build a beautiful terrain model. Other young soldiers would drift by and mock us. "Don't worry about them," I'd tell my Marines. "This is going to be something we can be proud of. I've never seen a terrain model this good."

The next day, Lieutenant Colonel Halloway could hardly have been happier. He called it the best terrain model he'd ever seen, and went out of his way to praise the intelligence section. I beamed with pride and looked over at my Marines, who were still disgruntled at having had to build the model at all.

That evening, a buddy of mine, Lieutenant Dawson, sat on the dirt next to me and lit a cigarette. He'd been with the unit a few years and was about to be promoted to captain. Just a few months before, he'd returned from a deployment to Afghanistan where his actions had won him the recognition of all the captains in the battalion.

"What the fuck is the yarn?" he asked.

"Oh, right," I replied. "The yarn represents the phase lines of the operation. You can see Phase Line Green over on that side all the way to Phase Line Red over near the mountain."

"No," he said, confused. "I mean, what the fuck? Like, did you go buy yarn?"

"Yeah," I replied cautiously.

"Like when we were in garrison for a week, you went to the store and pulled out your credit card and bought yarn?"

"I put it on the battalion account, but yeah," I said, not knowing why I was starting to feel rather embarrassed. "What's your point?" Dawson took a long drag on his cigarette.

"Why?" he asked, as if I weren't a native English speaker. "Why the fuck would you buy yarn? Why the fuck did you build this thing? Do you think a lot of Medal of Honor winners bought yarn?"

"Oh, well, Lieutenant Colonel Halloway—"

"I don't give a fuck about Halloway. Of course he wants yarn!" Dawson put out his half-smoked cigarette. "Of course he wants a terrain model built to scale, covered in arts and crafts! He doesn't have to build it."

"Dawson," I reasoned. "I agree with you, but what am I supposed to do? Say, 'No, sir'?"

"Yes."

"I can't say no. He's my commander," I replied, frustrated. "There's nothing I can do."

"I don't know, man," he said, changing to a more conciliatory tone. "If you excel at stupid shit, you're going to keep being tasked with stupid shit. Halloway doesn't just need you to execute orders; he needs you to help him understand the best use of his assets. Is this the best use of his intelligence analysts?"

Dawson paused and smashed the cigarette farther into the dirt. We sat in silence. "Shit," he said finally. "Never in my life have I gone to the store to buy some fucking yarn." He laughed. I laughed too. He stood up to leave. "You're good," he said definitively. "You'll get it."

I was safely down from the high of pleasing Halloway and thought a long time about my conversation with Dawson. I still felt the yarn was a nice touch, but I took his point. I'd been a good manager and a terrible leader.

In Part One I noted Julius Caesar's famous remark that he'd rather be first among the barbarians than the second man in Rome. Building the best terrain model was like being king among the barbarians. I wanted to be back in Rome. I'd won a contest that wasn't worth competing in. As little as it matters why you lose, it matters very much where and how you win.

YOU'LL NEVER GO TO WAR

From the day I'd met him, Lieutenant Colonel Halloway told me I'd never deploy. He smiled as he said it, amused by my naivete. "I've got you for three years," he said, holding three fingers up. "You'll never go to war. So get it out of your head."

Of all the other artillery battalions like mine, none had an intelligence officer. I'd always wondered why, until one day Halloway invited me to lunch at the Officer Club, a restaurant on base.

When he issued the invitation, I wondered whether we might be turning a corner. At lunch, though, he looked distracted as I tried to make conversation. He ignored me and searched the room, his eyes finally lighting on a group of colonels seated at a table across the room. "Get up," he interrupted, still looking at them.

Halloway was all smiles when we arrived at their table. He even put his arm around me. They invited us to sit. Halloway talked about what a great intelligence officer I was, how we were the only artillery battalion to have one. He talked about how we spent six of every seven weeks in the field, how that meant we dropped more bombs than any other unit. He was selling. Hard.

While Halloway was putting on his show, the colonel sitting next to me asked about my background. As I replied, he shook his head. "And now you're his prop," he said, almost to himself.

When I returned to my unit, I went to the executive officer and told him about the incident. He shook his head and closed the door. Then he revealed that I hadn't been slated for an artillery battalion in the first place. Halloway had pulled a tricky maneuver the week I'd finished my training. He thought that being the only battalion with a full staff would give him an argument to deploy.

Halloway's scheming was a sobering lesson to me. I was his dead weight. I was his faceless subordinate. I finally saw just how ugly my own ambition could be when it sacrificed the people around me. He and I, it turned out, wanted the same thing: to deploy to combat. We could have worked together. But Halloway was a loner. He showed me what it looked like to scheme alone. It looked ruthless and hollow.

The lion in me may have wanted loyalty to my Marines and acceptance in the job I'd been given, but it wouldn't stand to be treated like a pawn. My *thumos* was showing its teeth now. I wanted out and I was ready to let my mind do whatever was necessary.

My plan took several intense months. I made myself absolutely ready to deploy on a moment's notice. I lived in my truck instead of getting a lease. I kept all of my gear and belongings packed. I even went to the hospital to get the long series of shots needed to go to the Middle East. I also began forming relationships with every other intelligence officer I could find, trying to get someone to pull me. Finally, I got new orders to a team bound for Afghanistan to train the Afghan National Army (ANA).

When Halloway found out, he first tried to get the orders canceled. When that didn't work, he volunteered me for a course in Nepal so that I'd leave for a month and wouldn't be able to deploy. He called around, he begged his commander, he did everything he could to stop me. But without a coalition, he was powerless. He called me into his office, put me at parade rest, and screamed in my face. "You think you can backdoor me, motherfucker?!" he yelled.

I'd never heard a lieutenant colonel yell something like that, and never would again. But I knew he wasn't really yelling at me. He was yelling in frustration that he'd been beaten in his own game. I was going to war.

Chapter 4

STRANGERS WITH NO CANDY

ENTOURAGE

Going to the war in Afghanistan felt like I'd finally made it. I thought about how I'd embraced my anger and aggression, how I'd started to understand and shape my *thumos*. I thought about Socrates's hydra, lion, and small man, and how far I'd come in getting them to work together. I was surrounded by desert, but my life was anything but beige.

Initially I'd started to chart my own path independently, embracing the idea of Me Against the World. I wanted something independent. I wanted my own skills, my own adventure. I wanted to earn my spurs and make a name for myself. If I was going to fail, I wanted no one to blame but myself.

In those days, I used to imagine the peak position as a solo performance. I was going to prove all the naysayers wrong. But as I started my adventure, part of that anger and resentment changed shape. Some people, I realized, were on my side. Koch was a friend. Others stood for things that I was inherently against. They weren't just people I wanted to prove wrong. They were enemies. My understanding of Us was larger than my initial Me. And the vague World that I'd set out to conquer became a clear Them that I was against. My anger was focused; so was my loyalty.

But as I joined my new team and headed to Afghanistan to become an advisor for the Afghan Army, I found that my adventure was about to expand yet again.

When we first started our work, I'd thought that the growing network of partners, contractors, mercenaries, and allies was peculiar to my advisor team. As I've come to learn, though, this is a native part of any adventure. Bands go on to have managers, agents, and opening acts. Sports teams have doctors, marketing teams, and fans. A start-up has suppliers, potential acquirers, and integrators. Politics may be the clearest example, where the primaries deliver messaging to your team and the general election needs to build a coalition out of all those without a side. Whatever you build, you can't seem to grow without having to deal with weak links.

The trouble with the strangers you have to work with is that they'll never be as much like you as your team. You'll have to build trust with people you otherwise wouldn't. They may not share your values; they may not share your goals. Often, they don't even share the same language. Sometimes, the same contractor working for you is working for your competition. It's confusing and hard.

Although the particular groups are always different, the principles are the same. It's princely work to build an alliance that can win. It requires constant mediation and negotiation. To build trust is neither a checklist nor an ominous cloud. It takes upkeep and maintenance. There's more structure and mechanics to the building of trust than I'd ever imagined.

In this first deployment to Afghanistan, I risked becoming irrelevant in the enterprise, lost in the general malaise of weak alliances. I needed to learn how to create my own authority, how to get everyone else to respect my homemade legitimacy. I had to learn how to use that authority to strengthen our alliance and protect my team.

I'd thought that becoming a teammate had been difficult, but there was an even larger challenge in trying to wrangle all the disparate people and moving parts of a large coalition. It called on everything I'd learned about how my mind, *thumos*, and appetites worked together. I'd started to see the power of *thumos*, the lion, not just in disagreement and conflict, but in protecting its own. Now I would have to learn how *thumos* could turn strangers into friends.

TOO MANY BULLETS

Day two in Afghanistan, and we'd already hit our first IED. The bomb had been placed in an otherwise empty desert. Why some Taliban member had thought to drive all the way out there to bury one was beyond me.

Hitting an IED wasn't a surprise. I must have trained the response to it a hundred times. Driving over a bomb so early confirmed what I thought I knew about the war I was getting into, where the enemy tied our shoelaces together with our own rules of engagement.

As advisors to the Afghan National Army, our 20-man team lived on their base with them. The advisor team before us had carved out a corner just for Marines that they called Camp Alamo, named after their chances of survival, if the Afghans ever decided to attack.

Advising sounded easy enough from training in California—drink lots of tea with them and avoid talking about religion—but the reality was proving harder. The Afghans had seen this too many times. Advisors would come in, enthusiastic to jump-start operations, then slowly lose motivation, spending the rest of their deployments waiting out the clock in their tents. I was just the latest of their mom's boyfriends, showing up with a baseball glove and calling them "champ."

After just three weeks, this lack of trust proved to be much more of a threat than I'd imagined. One of our Afghan partners took his rifle up into a watchtower and had started firing wildly, trying to kill members of our team. This wasn't an IED we'd hit on the road. This was a gun in our living room. We weren't prepared for this.

One of the translators ran through the camp screaming, "Too many bullets! Too many bullets!" Over the radio, we heard a report that another translator was bleeding and being rushed to medical. The Afghan Army quickly disarmed and detained the attacker. Our own response, however, was still in chaos.

Most of the team had run toward the fight. As we scrambled for information, every Marine tried to be the hero. We didn't know that the shooter had been detained, and we didn't know whether he'd acted alone. Finally, we gathered together and found that no one had been shot. The bleeding translator had cut his leg while running away.

I'd gone to the war thinking it was a deadly game of cat and mouse, and that it could be won by being competent and lethal. But after that first insider attack, I started to appreciate how betrayal could be a far more malignant force than a few incoming bullets. More Afghans could be turned by such an incident, whether they'd just been waiting for their opportunity or whether some latent hostility got triggered. Other Afghans, their pockets lined with bribes, would be willing to look the other way. In such an unstable situation, friends, enemies, and strangers weren't so easy to tell apart.

We, too, were off balance. A plainly external enemy would have had us quickly banding together, but an insidious internal one tore us apart. Every Marine seemed to have a different interpretation of events, yet everyone was angry: angry with the Afghans, angry with each other, angry with the Marine Corps that put them there in the first place.

At first glance, anger can seem brutish and thuggish. It looks like the color red, spewed all over whatever canvas is within its reach. But there was a lot more going on within our team and within the Afghan Army than a straightforward tantrum.

Matters of trust were at stake. Who were we to each other? Who was ready to leave? Who was ready to fight? Who among us would die? Anger is the part of us that will hold people accountable for betrayal, incompetence, negligence, unreliability, and deception. It's also the part of us that protects the things we love, defends boundaries, and stands loyal against all apparent reason.

Getting shot at by our allies was a dramatic example, but this sort of incident happens to everyone. It's the moment you catch someone you love in a lie, when you can see your child is keeping something from you. It's when your friends leave you out of a social gathering or your business partner leaves you out of a decision they know you'd want to weigh in on. Is this how we're treating each other now? Am I going to let them get away with that? If they aren't ashamed, if they aren't sorry, is this what the new reality will look like?

Moments like these feel like a glitch in the system, when it turns out that the world isn't what we thought it was. The mind will analyze such things and can be helpful. But it's our heart, with anger as its arm, that will decide how we feel about it and what we'll do.

THE HIERARCHY

Before I'd joined the Marines, I'd expected the hierarchy to offer the clearest orders that I'd ever experienced. My commanding officer could tell me whatever he wanted me to do, and I'd do the same to my Marines. I also thought that war would have clear boundaries and easily identifiable enemies.

What I found instead was confusing. New written orders and policies would come at least every day from higher headquarters that dictated the way I ran things. I had a commanding officer named Colonel Wrenforth, who knew me exactly as well as his other 5,000 Marines. In my patrols and operations, I had to clear things through Colonel Harris, whom I hadn't met. Then I also reported to Lieutenant Colonel Treglia for my mission of advising Afghans.

Major Thorne didn't like lieutenants and made sure we knew it. He insisted I follow the lead of my older Marines, regardless of rank. He also told my Marines they didn't have to listen to me because I had no experience.

When we were off the base, patrolling, I was in charge of all the Marines, but on base, everyone had different functions. On any given day I had at least five people ordering me on what to do, and virtually no Marines I could task who wouldn't have some excuse for getting out of it.

We had six captains who outranked me but who also came with varying reputations. I didn't report to Captain Shinn, but I wanted to. Of the others, Major Thorne called one pair Tweedle Fuck and Tweedle Fucker, and those were the nicest pet names in the group. I wasn't sure if I had to listen to them.

The Afghan side was even more confusing. Their army had ranks and hierarchy, but they were also split by tribes. A major might order a captain to do something, but if one was Pashtun and the other was Tajik, you might have an issue. If one was an Uzbek, all hell might break loose.

The enemy was worst of all. To defeat our mission of training the Afghan Army, the Taliban worked to get their soldiers to attack us. Some of those soldiers had been Taliban who joined the army. Others had joined to fight the Taliban but were later convinced to switch sides. And some hadn't switched sides, but were sympathetic to the Taliban as Muslims who were skeptical of the mostly Christian United States Marines sent to teach them.

Following orders in that environment was like a game of Twister, with all of us trying to balance while wrapped around each other. The hierarchy looked clean on a PowerPoint slide, but was really more like a game of Chutes and Ladders. Many of the Marines wrote off our tour as a joke because of the wild structure, but to me, this was a master class in authority.

My Afghan team was a classic case of diffused responsibility, where success had many fathers but failure was always an orphan. It was where I learned that people are generous with other people's money, that the left hand doesn't know what the right hand is doing, and that people will try anything so long as it doesn't threaten their reputation. It's also where I learned that doing good and impactful things came more from understanding how to work in the big enterprise than from having novel ideas. Anyone navigating complex in-laws, high school, or the PTA knows these rules well.

My lesson was plain: If the military hierarchy isn't clear, then no hierarchy is. No one can simply give you power any more than they can give you legitimacy. At most, you can hope for a title and a blessing. The rest is up to you. Power must be earned or taken, and then kept. Whoever put you into power quickly becomes your biggest threat to being removed from power. Hierarchies weren't as simple as they looked on the org chart.

This all had me thinking much differently about how Socrates's hydra, lion, and small man worked together. At first reading, it had looked like a smooth and relatively simple hierarchy: The small man ruled the lion and the lion and the small man together ruled the hydra. But even that wasn't clear-cut either. Consent of the governed, checks and balances, and trust between the parts was critical to making them work together. Order wasn't a top-down mandate; stability came from a negotiated balance.

FRUIT BY THE FOOT

In the Afghan Army, bribes were the currency of the realm. We didn't offer cash—at least, not outright. But drones, weapons, and vehicles were always on the table. My first Afghan meeting was with Major Tawoos, the intelligence officer for our Afghan unit and who was rumored to be one of the most corrupt men in the battalion.

My predecessor had been too high-minded to make deals with Tawoos, disgusted by his crookedness. But I didn't care if Tawoos embezzled a pile of riches, so long as it made the Afghan Army better fight the Taliban. I was going to have him eating out of the palm of my hand. Major Tawoos was going to be my puppet.

We arrived in his tent at night. Most tents were beige and empty, but Tawoos had filled his with acquired riches: tables, colorful rugs, even a TV. In the center of the rug sat a dozen plates, each with different fruits and nuts on them.

"Salaam alaikum!" Major Tawoos said happily. He was dressed in camouflage sweatpants and a T-shirt that framed his potbelly. Just under his balding head were eyes aimed in two completely different directions. This was going to be easier than I thought.

We sat on the ground cross-legged with Major Tawoos as he welcomed me and the two men with me—my staff sergeant, Watson, and my translator, John. As he spoke, though, neither eye was looking at us. Instead, he stared at his feet as he rubbed them without shame.

He had no socks on, which the thick calluses on the bottoms of his feet indicated was part of his standard dress. His toenails were long and colored like the before photo in an ad for athlete's foot. I stayed polite, waiting for my time to make a deal. Watson stared, unable to hide his horror.

After we'd conversed for a while, back and forth like politicians—"Ours will be a great partnership, sir, one that will show strength through trust"—Major Tawoos's hands left his feet and dug into the food before us. He fondled the grapes, letting them fall through his fingers.

We'd been polite and I'd put in the necessary small talk. Now was time for business. But before I could begin, Major Tawoos cut me off. John translated.

"Major Tawoos say he is completely open to you, sir," John translated. "He say all his intelligence is yours to take just as all this food." Major Tawoos then popped a grape into his mouth, holding out the rest for me to take.

I was taken aback. It would be impolite to turn the foot grapes down, especially when we were trying to establish trust. Major Tawoos was using my manners against me like a weapon. These grapes represented the sharing of information, the beginning of our partnership. He smiled as I took one in my hand. Watson wasn't able to manage a smile, eyeing his grape like a cyanide pill.

"More. More," Major Tawoos insisted. Watson looked at me, suggesting that I say something. I glanced back a silent order to fill his mouth. We each chewed in resentment.

Many fruits later and deeper in conversation, I tried my best to casually mention the operations I wanted. Major Tawoos ignored me, changing the subject. We left with full stomachs and empty hands.

I was humiliated. Every time Watson retold the story to our team, Major Tawoos's feet got dirtier and I got meeker. I'd gone in thinking that Major Tawoos was a simple character, that he'd be easy to manipulate. Reading the reports of his corruption, I'd envisioned a sort of greedy cartoon character holding bags with dollar signs on them. Instead, I was his puppet, forced to eat grapes topped with toe jam.

My interaction with Major Tawoos was a new sort of game, one I wasn't used to. My peers, subordinates, and commanders in the States had all been reasonably clear relationships. But working with an allied army was different. And the game that Major Tawoos was playing with me, where we each tried to get the upper hand, was different entirely.

PLAYING WITH BOUNDARIES

I was reminded of the games I'd played with my son, Michael, when he was just a baby. He loved toys, but would eventually get bored and start showing interest in everything that wasn't a toy. My coffee mug was a favorite every morning, as were the remote and my computer.

That, too, was a different kind of game, a moral game about transgressing boundaries. He would score a point when he touched something he wasn't supposed to. I scored a point when I stopped him from touching something he shouldn't. I would stop his hand from touching my keyboard and he'd wince. Just after, though, he would pretend to reach the computer again, laughing very hard when he saw my face.

Like the game with Major Tawoos, we were exploring boundaries together. Michael kept trying to find new things to pull on, put in his mouth, or climb. As he did, I had to keep making judgment calls as to whether I should let him explore, or if it was too risky. He'd touch my computer keyboard and I'd decide the contents were too valuable for him to potentially delete. But when he touched my screen, I'd pause and wonder how much damage he could really do. A few hundred dollars, but no content. I'd let him touch the screen.

I could have won the game tyrannically with my mind, setting up physical barriers that would simply keep restricted items out of his reach. But that wouldn't really be playing anymore. To set up such boundaries, the moral game would change from a game between responsive souls to a test of disconnected cleverness.

I could put my computer on a shelf; he would figure out how to climb to the shelf. I could block a doorway; he would learn to push through. Such cleverness has its uses, but in this case it would be all just calculated and physical. He and I would fail to play morally.

I could have removed all boundaries and let him touch, grab, and pull whatever he wanted, setting his hydra free to do whatever it wanted. Touching a knife, he would find that it hurts and would learn not to touch the knife. But that too would just be physical.

In fact we were playing a thumotic game, one that needed to happen invisibly, manifest only in our faces as we responded to the other's moves. The transgression of boundaries is an act of the lion, despite its often being of questionable honor. It's the same game I'd played as a teenager when a friend dared me to climb over a barbed wire fence. After I did, I climbed right back over. Still, the line had been crossed and became my achievement. I was enlarged from it somehow.

St. Augustine understands the same when he recalls a time as a boy that he stole pears with his friends. They weren't particularly hungry and the pears didn't even taste very good. But he was still excited to steal them, and knew that he wouldn't have been as excited if he'd been stealing alone. He wonders why we transgress.

Human beings are built to test and break boundaries. We delight at exploration and expansion. Neighbors argue when the property marker is a few inches off. Yet we also do this with honor and permission all the time. It's how we build our authority.

Authority comes from what the people around you will allow you to do. It's the invisible game that Michael and I played. You transgress a boundary, perhaps something as simple as telling someone to get you a coffee. If they do it, even after some pushback or banter, they've ceded some small permission for you to do it again. All day long, we're playing these games with our kids, neighbors, and coworkers. We're testing our authority and giving our permission.

At my first company, I won permission through constant argument and debate. I was very careful to do and say things that I thought could be defended, so that when I was challenged, I'd dig into my arguments. I didn't win all of them by a long shot, but soon my employees were sick of having to go 12 rounds on a small point. They started choosing their battles very carefully, giving me permission to do what I liked. When I suggested we begin selling robots in Europe, I had a complicated argument I'd planned and knew inside out, but I never had to use it. Although many on my team disagreed, they knew that I wouldn't have brought it up if I weren't prepared to defend it.

After a few years, that authority had grown to the point that I might have been able to tell everyone that our new dress code would be pink tank tops every day and no one would have said anything. My general strategy had been a great exercise in understanding how permission gives way to authority, but it ended up having its own lessons in the downsides of tyranny. I'd learned how to compel my team to do what I wanted, but I'd failed to learn how best to put their talents to work.

The legitimacy that's won in these games becomes something more real than titles or job descriptions. The back and forth ignores the rule book, yet establishes house rules nonetheless. It's just how everyone plays together. We often think of authority as something mysterious and suspicious. But it's actually not mysterious at all. We make and break authority every day.

Raising kids is almost all about what you let them get away with. Fights in marriage are almost always about someone wanting permission and the other wanting to restrict it. It's how company cultures are created and how team dynamics are established. When the small man allows the hydra to act without challenge one night, he shouldn't be surprised when the hydra begins where he left off the next. To get authority back, we need to be ready to enforce a boundary.

In the new world I was entering, where rank was discounted and hierarchies unclear, this sort of game was the way to become someone. I'd been beat badly by Tawoos in our first round, but I was intent on learning how to play better.

ARMORED OFF

About a week after my team was shot at, higher headquarters issued new guidance for how advisor teams were to defend against insider attacks. I was excited to read it. The shooting had turned so much upside-down, I was happy to have some tangible plans for what we could do to stop it from happening again.

The new policies traded building trust for bodily protection. Every Marine was to carry two weapons and wear full body armor. One out of every two Marines was to act solely as a bodyguard. As I read over the guidelines, I grew more frustrated at every page.

Despite their study of the data gathered after every attack, higher headquarters seemed to minimize the issues of trust and betrayal that were obvious to anyone on the ground. I went to Captain Shinn and explained my concerns to him.

"You think the Pentagon got it wrong?" he asked, as if I'd just reported gambling in Casablanca. This was nothing new to Shinn, nor did it present a dilemma to him. He went immediately to the actionable response: "So what are you going to do different?"

I'd been so focused on what was wrongheaded about the policy from headquarters that I hadn't thought at all about what a better solution might be. "Well, sir," I said, hoping to spare myself from embarrassment. "When the soldier shot at us, the ANA had him detained in minutes. So I think we should focus more on building the trust with the soldiers who can protect us than on the tactics for stopping a rogue soldier."

"It's almost like you're saying," he said as if I'd just given evidence of a major conspiracy, "that as advisors we should build relationships with the Afghans and work together." His eyes widened with sarcasm as if he'd solved an even bigger mystery. "I wonder if the Afghans could even warn you of threats, since they belong to the culture, speak the language, and actually know the soldiers."

To Shinn, this had been the obvious starting point. Despite his mocking of my discovery, I was proud to be on the right track. He tasked me with developing specific ways of building greater trust with the Afghans, yet he also warned me not to ignore a tactical response.

The next day, I went back to Shinn with a new plan. The cultural divide was large and practices that were normal to the Afghan Army—particularly their corruption and their harsh treatment of servants—were never going to be accepted by a team of US Marines. Like a family avoiding politics at Thanksgiving, though, we'd overlook our controversial differences by focusing on food, TV, and sports. Shinn helped me work through the details.

The Marine Corps' response was thumotic in a fundamental way. Our allies shot at us? Then treat them like enemies. Armor up; it's Us v. Them. What we were encountering now, however, was the trouble with strangers. We needed to expand our allies and work with partners, but without a clear Us and a clear Them, it wasn't obvious who might be a friend and who might be an enemy. We needed a different form of anger than what I was seeing, one that was less rigid, less limiting.

Though a few of the Afghans were probably friends and others secret enemies, the majority of the strangers were prepared to become either. It was our job to win them over while defending against any hidden enemies. Shinn recognized the need for defense but was willing to take on the princely and political task of building an alliance. That needed more than giving orders and closing ranks.

UNRULY JADES

Before I joined the Marines, I'd thought of command and leadership as simple givens. My Marines would be there to do as I told them. It was a military hierarchy, after all. My greatest challenge would be to outwit the enemy, directing obedient troops against them. In the aftermath of the shooting, however, the full scale of the larger challenge had started to emerge. I realized that I was living out a lesson I'd first encountered in Shakespeare's *Richard II*.

Richard II opens with a chivalrous duel between two of King Richard's dukes. But the audience is puzzled when Richard ends the fight just as it begins. While the two knightly lords were prepared to fight to the death, Richard chooses instead to banish them both from England. The trouble comes later when the banished Bolingbroke—Richard's own cousin—raises an army and returns to attack him.

King Richard's first response to *thumos* was: Suppress it; get rid of it. He doesn't seek a way to mediate the conflict or to build trust back among his dueling lords, whom he treats more like squabbling children. He seems unconcerned with keeping their loyalty or preserving their strength for England. Instead of the hard and skillful work of breaking horses, he simply sends two of his strongest away. Mediation and negotiation aren't in Richard's toolbox. He's never seen the need for them.

Having been king since he was a child, Richard hasn't known a life where he wasn't on the throne. And to him and most of England, his kingship wasn't a mere accident. He comes from a line of kings, all of whom were believed to be divinely appointed. Richard is God's minister on earth, acting with absolute power and answering only to Him.

As the divinely appointed monarch, King Richard has the authority to command England without negotiation or accommodation. Disobedience isn't just an act of treason; it's a defiance of God and a repudiation of His grace. Richard sees only the glory of his high station and the lowly world of his subjects below. He believes that everyone should gladly warm to his splendid majesty, as flowers welcome the sun.

He doesn't see the danger of banishing *thumos*. Rather than making good use of Bolingbroke, who clearly has much to offer, Richard exercises his prerogative to remove him from England. There's a serious cost to dishonoring proud men. But as is common in weaker leaders, Richard takes Bolingbroke's allegiance to the crown's authority for granted.

When Bolingbroke storms back from exile at the head of an army, intent on taking the throne and setting England to rights, Richard is shocked. Even worse, almost all of England is willing to join Bolingbroke in rebellion. Richard, whose rule was supposed to be godlike, is suddenly fragile and human. He's forced to surrender the crown.

Bolingbroke becomes the new king, crowned King Henry IV. But his victory sets a dangerous precedent, one that fundamentally changes the kingship in England. If he can take the throne rather than inherit it, what's to stop anyone else from doing the same? Crowns that are easy to take are difficult to hold. He's nothing special, just a politician, a point of equilibrium in a delicate trade-off of interests. His realm is the messy, mundane world in between the high heavens and the low earth.

After we'd been shot at from within our own walls, I began to see more clearly the fragility of even legitimate command. I had no tasking authority over the Afghan Army. I didn't speak the same language. Not even the Marines I worked with were mine to task as I pleased. Long ago I'd imagined that as a leader of Marines I'd be commanding as Richard did. I was quickly learning that it was Bolingbroke's challenge I faced instead: how to translate authoritative power into the tangled circumstances and competing interests of real time.

SNARLING AT STRANGERS

I was invited to question the soldier who'd shot at us. Three weeks into my tour, Afghanistan still felt strange enough that I didn't take the shooting personally. I didn't need him to feel pain or to feel sorry. All I really wanted was information for the stacks of reports I had to fill out. But when I looked at him more closely, I suddenly felt compelled to ask new questions.

Instead of asking when he'd developed the plan, if he was working with anyone else, or if he'd been approached by the Taliban, I asked where he was from. I asked why he'd joined the army. I asked what he thought of the war.

A billboard of an Afghan soldier behind a rifle in his small town had prompted him to join the army. Faith was at the center of his life and he thought of himself as a Muslim first, then a soldier, then an Afghan. He didn't have any strong hatred of the Taliban or the Americans.

Earlier that day, he'd wandered into a tent where some soldiers had acquired a small TV from the Marines. He'd never seen a TV before. The news was on and he heard a story about an American who'd made a movie that mocked Muslims. He was incensed. Why should he fight his fellow Muslims in the Taliban? Why should he partner with infidels?

No one had paid him. He hadn't caved to Taliban

intimidation. The day before, he'd been indifferent. In five minutes, the TV had convinced him that God wanted something different from what the Afghan generals did. This wasn't just a news clip to him. It was an ancient war. He'd chosen sides in that war long before he put on a uniform. He stood with God.

To *thumos*, unfamiliar people are threatening. It doesn't take much to provoke a warning snarl and not much more to deserve a bite. *Thumos* puts you on trial and demands evidence before it lets you in. It's the look of your first date's father when you say you'll have her home by 10.

It wasn't just the shooter. None of the Afghans were quite sure of what we were up to, why we'd left the comfort of America to join them in a forbidding desert. We spoke a different language, had different gestures, and held different things dear. We were strangers. They were skeptical.

The soldier transgressed a serious boundary the day he fired on our team, perhaps even a sacred one. Attacking a partner, breaking a covenant, and trapping your guest were all things *thumos* doesn't like. *Thumos*, the lion, defender of integrity and honor, wants to be a steadfast partner. But *thumos* was also a transgressor, a breaker of boundaries. It was the final push the shooter needed to climb the tower.

This dual nature of *thumos*, both a defender and an offender, was hard for me to grasp. But looking back, I understood it was why I'd been comfortable about going behind Halloway's back to get my deployment in the first place. To *thumos*, a handshake is a contract, but if that contract turns out to have been negotiated in bad faith, the lion will be the first to attack. In the deadly game of boundaries we were playing, *thumos* was transgressor and protector at once. Just as it sent the shooter to betray my team, it was what drove us to reestablish the boundary. *Thumos* is what denies the permission.

But this didn't need to become a new war. Shinn was showing me that *thumos* could also form a new partnership. We didn't need to become their brothers, or even their neighbors. We didn't need to solve the Islam–infidel divide once and for all. For the success of our mission, we just needed to cross over from threatening strangers to accepted guests.

Chapter 5

YOU CATCH MORE FLIES WITH MONEY

A GOAT IN SHEEP'S CLOTHING

Even before we'd been shot at, the threat of insider attacks hung over us all. One of the advisor teams we were relieving was going home having lost one of their Marines to a similar attack. A few days into our own mission, we had no rapport or relationship to fall back on, just plain evidence of the deadly threat to our lives and a year ahead of questionable partnership. With just 20 of us and hundreds of them, we knew they couldn't all be against us. But all it took was one.

I felt lost. I'd wanted to face the problem of the Taliban head-on. I'd wanted to direct my *thumos* and intelligence at the enemy, returning home with stories of clever tactics and glorious achievements. Instead, I was like an unwanted foreign exchange student trying to make friends. Not quite the makings of an illustrious career.

To make matters worse, it was the beginning of Ramadan—"Afghan Christmas," as our translators dubbed it. During the six weeks of Ramadan, the Afghans wouldn't eat or work while the sun was up. At night they feasted and celebrated. The Taliban took credit for the spikes in insider attacks during Ramadan, saying we were in a religious war. But seeing the skinny Afghans get even skinnier with fasting, I wondered if I was in a battle against low blood sugar.

Ramadan looked like a good opportunity to bond with our Afghan partners, but there was a serious impediment: We hadn't been invited. I asked my translator, John, a native Afghan, if there was a polite way for me to ask them to invite us. John confirmed that asking for an invite was as rude in Afghanistan as it was in America. He proposed a further principle: If you're going to crash a party, you'd better bring a good bottle of wine. His suggestion was to buy some sheep for slaughter and just show up at their celebration as though our invite had been lost in the mail.

I took his advice and began planning. I tasked Lieutenant Turner with sorting out a kitchen to kill and cook the sheep, and Haberer with finding vegetables and sides. Then I got approval for "Operation Black Sheep" from headquarters, which raised some eyebrows and lowered their expectations for our success. We negotiated the purchase of five sheep from a wanderer who offered to deliver them right to our gate, and we paid him in advance. I'd come to Afghanistan for war; today, I was a party-planner in camouflage.

The next morning, though, we got stood up. After all our planning, I'd lost $200 to a vagrant shepherd. The Afghan soldiers would celebrate without us. The lower-level soldiers, noticing our absence, would confirm that we were outsiders, non-Muslims who were up to no good. John insisted that we wait at the gate even after the shepherd was several hours late. A sheep delivery suddenly felt like a matter of life and death.

Just as I'd lost hope, the shepherd approached the gate, pulling four unwilling goats with him. "See, sir?" John said. "He just has no clock. He thinks he is on time." The shepherd insisted that the goats were sheep and double-counted one of them, swearing there were five. I didn't care. I was getting used to a backward world. If I was calling this a military operation, I shouldn't have any trouble saying that four goats were five sheep.

We took the "sheep" and marched proudly toward the Afghan soldiers. Observing the pride we took in our gift, they smiled and welcomed us. John told them the story of how we'd been ripped off and we laughed together. We helped their cooks slaughter the goats, a harsh and bloody sort of bonding. Finally, we were invited to eat goat with them at dinner once the sun went down.

We sat surrounded by the Afghan soldiers, vulnerable to attack. Yet even without body armor on, the friendly rapport gave us confidence in our safety. Sure, we'd posted a hidden sniper who could kill anyone who so much as lifted his rifle—we were Marines, after all—but we knew that the trust we were building would protect us. On that night at least, we were safe.

I was proud of Operation Black Sheep, yet baffled by it too. Here we were, grappling with how to mitigate a real threat to our lives by bringing gifts to a party. It seemed absurd that a gesture like that could build something so grand as trust. Yet it worked. It was small, ridiculous, and doable, but it made a major impact. Trust had always felt like some untouchable, spiritual thing. But I was beginning to see that it had parts and gears. There was suddenly something workable about it.

I've since realized that thinking of trust as something ethereal and godly is an easy trap to fall into. On each of our birthdays in my family, my wife and I ask the kids what they love about the birthday boy or girl. Every time, we're amazed at how tangible the answers are. They remember drawings their sister gave them or when their brother helped them on their bike. Small acts build real trust.

Husbands everywhere wonder why their wives need flowers and dates, wanting them to see their love without the gifts. But a thoughtful act or her favorite chocolate becomes tangible evidence of his love. Showing up on time seems a matter of logistics to the husband but a sign of dependability to the wife.

Company C-suites agonize over why their employees haven't listened to their lectures on the company culture. But they're shocked to see that policy changes really do change behaviors. Oftentimes, a small note about a piece of feedback actually prompts the person to change how they act. Many take less than a minute to write!

Like King Richard, we can easily begin to believe that we're gods on earth, above the small, animal acts on the ground. We forget that those we love need reminders of that love, that there's a structure to trust, that we don't divinely deserve to be trusted. But such small acts become important evidence. For us in Afghanistan, it may have saved our lives.

GIFTS AND GRATITUDE

Years after that time in my advisory role with the Afghan Army, in a Harvard leadership class, I was reminded of how important simple trust can be at the outset of a relationship. We were watching sections of *12 Angry Men*, pausing for brief discussions between scenes. In one of those scenes, a juror offers the room a piece of gum. Everyone turns it down except Juror 8, the protagonist who's trying to convince everyone else to change their minds.

"What's with the gum?" our professor asked. All my 90 classmates sat silent. No one seemed to have noticed the small gesture. The offer of gum, though, meant a lot to me. I raised my hand.

"Juror 8 accepted the gum to win over the juror who'd offered it," I said. My professor raced across the room toward me, excited.

"Mike thinks Juror 8 is going to reverse the verdict of a murder trial by accepting a piece of Big Red!" he breathlessly yelled. Everyone laughed. "Wouldn't it be a better strategy to be *giving* people gum? To be *giving* people something instead of *taking* it?" he asked.

"No," I responded. "People like gifts, but they often only get you short-term gratitude. Accepting an offered gift—especially when everyone else turns it down—is the beginning of a partnership. It says, 'I see the value of what you're offering,' while at the same time it's a form of surrender. And most people respond by showing mercy, taking care of you instead." The class sat silent, waiting for the professor to enter his own verdict.

"All this for gum?!" he exclaimed, bringing on the laughter again.

"When I was deployed to Afghanistan," I said, provoking a few eye rolls but quelling the laughter, "accepting cups of chai was part of the strategy for protecting our lives. We were trained to accept every offer of food, drink, or gift made to us by the Afghans, for exactly this reason. When I accepted the chai or the candy, I had a good chance of learning some useful, potentially lifesaving intel in the conversation that followed."

"Yes," my professor said definitively, no longer playacting. "Accepting people's gifts has tremendous power. Asking people for something they have to give or valuing something they offer shows them that you think they're valuable. There's serious power in making yourself vulnerable. And ask people for *advice*?!" The class laughed at his inflection. "They'll drop everything they're doing to give you advice. People will get on a *plane* to give you advice! They'll fly across the country! On their own dime!"

He walked to the remote to begin the next scene, but paused to add, "You're all good with words. It's part of why you're here. But to achieve the things you're aiming for, you'd better start thinking more about what your actions say."

To this day, Lieutenant Colonel Treglia, my commander in Afghanistan, will say that the hardest thing he did on our tour was eat catfish out of the Helmand River. If I could go back in time, the first thing I'd change would be to eat more of my mother-in-law's food when I met her. I'd been blind for a long time to the importance of accepting gifts and to the disrespect of refusing them. As much as we sometimes hope to be above it, everyone hates to have an offer of theirs declined. We get irritated, angry. It's a core thumotic experience. All this for gum.

Even the smallest offers can be olive branches. There really is a fellowship that comes from breaking bread together. Yet so many of us find it so natural to say "No, thank you," not realizing that we're saying no to a small part of the person who's offering. Disagreement had been a new power when I'd needed to break away. Agreement and acceptance were proving just as strong when I needed to put things together.

NAVIGATING THE GRAY

Our early actions had turned the tide with the Afghans. They weren't openly hostile anymore, as some of them had been. But it wasn't going to be general goodwill that would protect us from more shootings. We needed friends. And we needed friends with information.

Lieutenant Monier was the third in command of the Afghans' intelligence section. The intelligence head was corrupt, his deputy inept. But Monier was sharp and discerning, and he also had heart. John trusted him. I needed him to trust me.

We'd interviewed so many prisoners that we knew what they were going to say better than they did. Many were teenagers, and we treated them accordingly. But today, our prisoner was no boy. He was a grown man, a real enemy. He'd attacked our patrol unprovoked. He'd planned to kill our soldiers. He wanted blood.

Usually when it came to questioning prisoners, I was the one holding back. Monier paid less heed to the rules of engagement, a common attitude of the Afghan officers. He was always wanting to do more than they allowed. It wasn't a point of contention exactly, but we noticed the gap. On this particular occasion, I allowed myself to be a bit more aggressive. I needed to do something outside the norm that would show Monier I wasn't a slave to my orders. This was my chance to prove that I could be trusted.

So, instead of my normal professional mode, I moved in very close to the prisoner and rattled out questions in quick succession—a pace the prisoner clearly hadn't planned on. John, translating, maintained my exact momentum and tone. I was going to have his full attention.

The prisoner had hidden his weapon after his attack, exploiting our mercy and expecting that he was now untouchable. But my posture made him wonder. He started to treat the questioning seriously. Monier laughed at the change. I was earning his trust, protecting my team.

That was when Thorne came in. He saw me and lost his mind. He screamed at me, grabbed me by the shoulder, and pushed me into an adjoining room. Holding me against the wall, he continued to shout. Monier could hear everything through the thin walls. In less than three minutes, Thorne had set me back more than three months.

When I walked back in, I was like some cocky teenager whose mom had just dragged him out of the room by his ear. It was so pitiful that even the cold-blooded prisoner seemed embarrassed for me. Monier, my partner, couldn't help grinning. Major Thorne, who was supposed to be on my team, had undermined me and thwarted my mission.

Later that day, I beat the side of the thick tent with my fist until my knuckles bled. My Afghan partners were trying to kill me, my enemies laughed at my restraint, and I'd been chewed out for looking dominant in a combat zone. No one was acting as I thought they should. Afghanistan was proving to be a fun house where every path forward was a surprising dead end and all the mirrors made me look like a fool.

That night, Captain Shinn found me and asked if I wanted to smoke a cigar. "I heard you played a little good cop, bad cop today," he said, smiling.

"Sir," I began, "Major Thorne—"

"Was a dick, right?" he said, finishing my sentence sarcastically. "Was that a new experience for you?"

"No, sir," I admitted. "But you know how hard it is to build rapport. I needed to win Monier over."

"So, to advise a foreign officer on the policies developed by the Marine Corps, you pretended you were on *Law and Order*," he concluded sarcastically.

"No, sir," I replied, losing my patience. "But without trust, the foreign officer won't let me *advise* him to the nearest bathroom."

"I see," he said. "So it's everyone else's fault." We smoked a minute in silence.

"Thorne was wrong anyway," I added, defending myself against an unspoken argument. "I talked to a JAG. I didn't break any rules."

"It's Thorne's job to keep you out of jail," he said, "the Taliban's job to kill you, and Monier's job to get as much as he possibly can out of you. But they're all more than their jobs. It's your job to figure that out."

I nodded. I'd been reducing everyone else to what I thought they should be doing, but the reality was much richer. I'd been trying to take a shortcut to building trust, trying to build trust by being clever. I wasn't going to manipulate my way to making friends.

"Oh, Lieutenant." He shook his head. We laughed at the absurdity of it all.

Years before, I'd been inspired by a general who'd said of Afghanistan, "This isn't checkers; this is chess." He'd delivered that line in a speech about how complex the wars had become. I was living out his point, yet I found that chess didn't seem right either. In chess, although the pieces move, they don't change. But Afghanistan was a game in which rooks sometimes moved diagonally, in a war without well-defined sides. It wasn't black and white pieces, just variations of gray.

ABSOLUTE POWER

Bolingbroke didn't grow up thinking that he would be king. Although one of the royals, and a man with a kingly temperament, he was still one branch of the family tree away. England didn't choose the best man for the job. God chose the heir. Richard was to be king, whether fit for the role or not.

As silly as that system sounded to me, having grown up in America, it had its merits. Richard was of good stock, his grandfather having been an excellent king and his father a revered leader and warrior. Perhaps more important, though, was his legitimacy. When there's only one heir and a single line of succession, there's one evident king. Everyone accepted that.

His monarchical legitimacy gave Richard extreme power. He could kill, banish, and tax his subjects as he pleased, and mostly not be challenged. But although he could treat all his subjects as servants if he liked, there was still a very powerful group of lords immediately below him, each with his own bloodline, lands, and armies.

While Richard's authority was paramount, it wasn't absolute. If he went too far outside the interests and wishes of his lords, they had serious practical recourse against him. Less than two centuries before, King John had been forced by his rebel barons to sign the Magna Carta, a set of limitations on the king that likely wouldn't have been ratified without the equivalent of a gun to his head.

Richard learns the hard way that all power is political. Keeping his lords or barons happy is job number one, because without their support, it doesn't much matter what job number two is. Bolingbroke raises an army to take the crown, but he doesn't need to use it. He has Richard in political checkmate.

It's a great if awkward victory for Bolingbroke. Without shedding the blood of his kinsman, he becomes the king of England, jailing Richard. As he does, though, his legitimacy becomes seriously contested. Richard isn't the only one who learns that all power is political. All of England has now seen behind the curtain.

The king isn't some anointed angel. He's just some guy. England learned what Japan would later learn when their emperor surrendered in World War II on the radio. After seeing him as a sort of divine hero, only in polished glimpses, his people now had a new question about him: Why's his voice so high-pitched?

As an advisor, I was obliged to forget my high theories of an officer's role and instead become a student of politics. I wasn't an absolute monarch, and neither the Marines nor the Afghans were my servants. The Afghans seemed unruly; my Marine leader, tyrannical. I needed to leverage the influence of an ambitious baron. I needed to build legitimacy as a leader with competence while winning their consent.

TURNING THEM INTO US

As a team of Marines who prided themselves on their strength, we had a lot of competitions in the makeshift gym we'd pieced together in one of the tents. Lieutenant Haberer, who had played football at the Naval Academy, was our strongest Marine. He was the record holder for most of the different lifts we tracked on a whiteboard.

One day, some of the captains were teasing Haberer

about his strength. They couldn't come close to his performance and were talking about him as a sort of alien whose records shouldn't count. My translator, John, was nearby and decided to join in. "Most of your scores are very good, sir," he said. "I could beat you at dead lift. But they very good."

Everyone suddenly perked up. Most of the translators were either short and malnourished or plump and waddling. But John was ripped. He stood just under six feet tall with an eight-pack and biceps that had earned him the nickname "John Rambo" with the last team. Still, most of the current team couldn't imagine that one of our translators might beat our strongest Marine.

They began laughing dismissively at the challenge, but John insisted that he could lift more. Haberer graciously admitted that his dead lift wasn't that great and that John might be able to beat his score. But the others wouldn't have it. Some kind of honor seemed to be at stake. They were angry at the very idea. "You could *not* beat Haberer," one of them said definitively. "Why do the translators exaggerate everything?"

With that, the Marines began other conversations. It seemed the issue had been decided. John was fuming, but dutifully held in his anger. He leaned over to me, his face in turmoil at the disgrace he'd just been forced to suffer. "Sir," he said, "I could beat it. I could."

I hadn't been eager to get in the mud with the pigs, but seeing John's distress, I spoke over the other conversations. "I think John could beat Haberer's dead lift," I said cockily. "Why don't we go to the gym?"

With grumbling from my fellow Marines, we went to our gym and loaded a bar just a bit heavier than the one Haberer had lifted. John warmed up with a few pull-ups, then looked at his angry audience. They didn't believe he could lift it. They didn't want him to lift it. They wanted John to accept that he wasn't one of us. "Go ahead, John," I said, reminding him he had a friend.

John gave his arms a final shake and grabbed the bar, ignoring the sneers. He had a look of utter determination and breathed heavily. Then he jerked the bar with every ounce of his strength. It didn't budge. The Marines began snickering. I quietly prepared myself to smooth over John's humiliation.

But John didn't stop pulling. And as his face turned completely red and the veins in his neck seemed about to pop, the bar began to lift. The tent went silent. Finally, he got the bar to the full height of the lift. His entire body was shaking. As he set the bar back down, a joyful smile came over his face. "See?" he said casually, unable to hide his excitement. "I tell you I could."

The contest in the gym had been born of competition and testosterone, but it was a defining moment for John and me. Marines tended to treat their translators as tools; I saw John as a partner. I didn't take his trust or loyalty for granted, but knew it was something I needed to earn, regardless of our relative positions.

The translators weren't malfunctioning machines that needed a good smack to get them working. The Afghans weren't cattle that needed herding. Too often, Marines saw advising as an engineering problem, with people who got in the way. But just as an aggressive part of us wants to categorize Us and Them, it's that same part that can turn Them into Us, that can turn strangers into friends.

THE PERMANENT DIFFICULTY OF TRANSLATION

For advisors, communication was mission critical. The gap between us and our Afghan partners—in culture, religion, and especially language—made us strangers. *Thumos* doesn't like strangers. *Thumos* protects one's own. In Afghanistan, I was faced with the challenge of making strangers into friends. Translators were the frayed rope bridge I needed to cross.

The Marines often mocked the Afghans' way of talking and I never thought much about it until one day I met an elegant Afghan colonel who was obviously speaking with great command of his language. Suddenly I saw my error. It was our translators who were making the mistakes in English. Of course it wasn't the Afghan soldiers who couldn't piece a clear sentence together.

Our translators, many of whom had little training in English, inadvertently made the soldiers sound like fools, saying things like, "I no know that, sir," or "General say sir he not happy." It was hard to respect someone's opinion when they hadn't mastered basic subject-verb agreement. Without basic respect, building trust or making friends was out of the question.

So, for a report on a large Afghan meeting I attended, I decided to do a better translation. Rather than passing the normal notes from the meeting that made the speakers sound like cavemen, I intended to show the speakers as they actually spoke. I took John with me, but rather than having him take notes, I recorded the meeting.

That evening, John and I sat down in my tent, listening to the recording together while he translated. After roughing out an initial rendition, I asked about the different rhetorical styles, based on the details of our first draft. We worked for hours revising the document, until all the grammar was correct and John agreed that our English captured something of the nature and nuances of the speakers. I even included footnotes to explain some of the passages that seemed to come out of left field.

The next morning, I awoke to find that our translation had been sent all over the country. Other translators who shared my frustration with the normal depiction of Afghan soldiers forwarded it around the country. It had gone all the way to the commander of the NATO International Security Force, who personally sent me a message to thank me for producing it.

Just as accepting the offered gum could be more powerful than giving it, I was learning that gaining the Afghans' trust began with our trusting the Afghans. With two potentially aggressive groups skeptical of each other, someone needed to make the first move. If we wanted to be accepted as guests, we needed to leave our muddy boots at the door.

The mocking of Afghan grammar didn't stop the day my report went out. Marines didn't suddenly think of our counterparts as eloquent or smart. But we started to see that we couldn't trust the Afghans if we kept painting them as inept and unreliable. We'd taken one small step toward thinking of them as people. With more movement there, I hoped the Afghans would begin to see us in the same light.

This lesson has helped me develop a strong habit: I don't

believe every report I hear. In my companies, employees often want to tell me about how their peers screwed up. Their exaggerations serve a few functions. They get to hinder a potential competitor for resources and praise. They get to look like they're the one who knows better. They get to draw a clear line between them and the person they're talking about.

It's amazing how easy it is to believe what you're told about someone. I used to fall for the trap all the time, not figuring out until much later that many reports had been completely inflammatory. Demonizing people who aren't right in front of you comes so naturally to us, even when they're your friends! You hear bad news and your lion is ready to pounce. It took years for me to learn that the lion should be defending instead.

INSIDE JOKES

One morning, a Marine came to my tent with the report of an Afghan soldier who'd threatened to kill Marines. It was my job to go question him, and I well knew that the rumor of an insider threat would already be buzzing around without confirmation. Any whiff of disloyalty from our Afghan partners resulted in a witch hunt from higher headquarters. I hurried to the detainee facility, hoping to add some facts to the story before it took off without them.

The soldier's cammies draped off him like a boy who'd been trying on his father's uniform. He couldn't have been more than 16. Before we'd arrived, zip ties on his wrists, he'd been laughing with his guards. When I got there, he was explaining to an Afghan officer that he'd made a joke that he just wanted to punch a Marine. He really didn't know what trouble he was in.

In the normal course of things, he'd have been designated card-carrying Taliban and put in jail within 24 hours. Another stat of saved lives. But I didn't believe it. This kid wasn't a double agent; he was just a goofball who didn't yet understand the world around him.

"You didn't say you wanted to punch the Marine," I casually interrupted. He looked down at the ground. "You know how I know?" I asked in a friendly tone. "Because you were making a joke. And it's not funny to joke about punching Marines. You didn't make that joke because that joke isn't funny, right?" The soldier looked up at me as John translated: "No."

"Of course not," I assured him. "You think I've never told a joke? I'm a laugh riot." I grinned. "John, tell him how funny I am or I'll kill you."

John laughed. "Yes, sir. I tell him." The soldier began to laugh a bit, quickly restraining himself when he saw the Afghan officer's scorn.

"You know what *is* funny, though?" I continued. "Jokes about *killing* Marines. I make jokes about killing my buddies all the time. In English we call it gallows humor. It's a time-honored tradition. Soldiers have been making jokes about killing each other since you guys kicked Britain's ass out of here." The Afghan officer smirked. The soldier controlled his giggle.

"I bet you had a good joke, too, didn't you?" I went on. John, understanding my angle, played the soldier perfectly, jostling him a bit and laughing contagiously as he translated. Soon, the soldier was laughing, too, and said something.

"Sir," John said, suddenly professional. "He say he did make a joke about killing a Marine."

I stayed in character, reassuring the soldier that it was OK to joke. "Khoob ast. It's good. Khoob ast." I went on in English, "I make jokes like that all the time. When I heard I had a soldier to question, I said, 'Couldn't you just shoot him and I'll go to sleep instead?'"

The soldier laughed, then began matching my story with his own. John relayed, "He say that he was going on patrol with all of his buddies and the Marines were there. He say they were all talking about shooting each other, so he jump in and say, 'Hey, everyone. Why we talk about killing each other when we have Americans here? If we kill anyone, we should kill them!'"

I let out a genuine laugh of relief. An actual joke. An actual gaffe. I'd heard enough jokes like it on patrol to know it was real. Just a dumb kid making a dumb joke. He wasn't going to kill any of us. I had what I needed for a report to headquarters. I hoped it wasn't too late to stop the rumors.

As we walked back toward our camp, John weighed in for the first time since talking to the soldier. "Good thing he does not work with Marines anymore. Good thing we got to him, sir." I didn't understand.

"John," I said. "He was just joking. Don't you believe him?"

"He is a false rogue," John responded, using the Elizabethan English I'd earlier convinced him was American slang.

"Sure," I responded. "But he's just being a jackass, right? He's a nice kid."

"If he don't know he shouldn't say *that* joke, he should not be around Marines," John concluded.

John didn't want the soldier around Marines because he didn't have the judgment yet to know not to make a joke about killing Marines on patrol. He didn't have the judgment to lie effectively under questioning, either. He wasn't a threat right now, but he'd shown himself susceptible to being turned by the wrong people. After debriefing John on the questioning more thoroughly, I changed my assessment.

I was able to correct the report before rumor got too out of control. But I also recommended that the soldier be transferred to a unit away from Marines, and he was. The incident sat with me a long time. He was a nice kid, but being nice wasn't enough to make for a faithful ally. Loyalty took strength. If tested by a Taliban recruiter, loyalty could even require guile. This soldier had neither. There was a difference between being nice and being good.

KING OF GRIEFS

When I'd first read *Richard II*, I'd thought the lesson was that Richard became a better king after he was deposed. In losing his crown, he learned humility. With his kingdom and his riches gone, he discovers that he can now rule over his griefs and feelings. Those cannot be taken from him. He finds freedom in his solitary prison cell.

As Henry IV, Bolingbroke becomes a prisoner to the crown. With the legitimacy of his rule under a permanent shadow, everyone who helped him seize it is a future contender. He sits atop a divided kingdom, negotiating with the fractured groups and malcontents for his entire reign.

Richard at least had majesty and he held himself too pure to win at a dirty game. Shakespeare seemed to be teaching me that simple virtue can't exist in politics. His Richard is given some of the most beautiful poetry in any of his plays. He's wise enough by the end to appreciate what he's lost.

Bolingbroke, on the other hand, can find no satisfying way through the consequences of his actions. He barely manages to quell the rebellions against him. He dies with England still in faction, yet to be united, and believing that even his own son is deceiving him. Richard ruled an England Shakespeare presents in flowing iambic pentameter. Much of Bolingbroke's England is shown in stilted, unmetered prose that audiences can't always understand. He may have become king, but no one quotes Bolingbroke as though his soul and character were of intrinsic interest.

Afghanistan felt like the fragmented world Bolingbroke came to rule. We didn't live by the same laws or agree on who was in charge. There was no common speech, no shared values. There was no legitimacy—just guns, threats, and death. Alliances were brief and honor was a joke. There was nothing to win, only a whole bunch of ways to lose.

It was there that I revised my understanding of Bolingbroke. Richard's confidence and conviction had looked admirable when I was safely studying on a college campus, but as I negotiated a broken world myself, I came to better appreciate Bolingbroke's grayer virtues.

His England was in disarray, yet he held it together well enough to hand off the country to his son. Rebellions threatened him until he died, but he still prevented anyone else from seizing the crown. While Bolingbroke doesn't make great speeches about majesty or ceremony, he plays out a more worldly wisdom. Mundane political life needs executors, princes who are able to handle belligerent factions and lying courtiers. Although it's not often attributed to him, Bolingbroke was the first to say that uneasy lies the head that wears a crown.

INVISIBLE ARMOR

For a team that had been attacked by their partners early on, wearing just our cammies was a bold statement. To visitors, and even to some of the Afghan soldiers, we seemed like idiots. We could have worn armor and posted visible guards. Instead, we relied on a show of vulnerability to protect us, a cloak of invisible armor. Every day we met with the Afghans was like a trust fall.

We used the same tactics kids trying to be popular in grade school might use. We'd play movies on the side of a tent, brought the Afghans gifts, took photos with them and hung them up. We also began to play regularly with them in their soccer and volleyball games, though always avoiding an American versus Afghan match. We even tried cricket, amusing the Afghans with our lack of skill and understanding of the game.

Over time, all of it helped build a greater sense of fellowship between our team and the Afghans we were there to advise. There would of course always be a significant gap.

Everyone accepted that. Yet we were still able to find much to respect about each other.

Many other advisor teams, going into full calculation mode in response to the general threat, suffered more green-on-blue attacks. We didn't. It may in the end have had nothing to do with goodwill or trust. Our safety may have just been luck. Still, for years after, usually in the middle of the night, I'd receive a call from an unrecognized number.

"Hello, Buck," the voice would say, using my nickname.

"Salaam Alaikum!" I'd reply.

"How . . . are you?"

"Khoob ast. Khoob ast."

"OK. OK. Goodbye."

It was Monier. Whenever he had access to a phone, he'd call, responding in his broken English to my butchered Dari. We didn't have any words of substance to say to each other, yet somewhere in our year together, we'd formed a real fellowship. Our team had been lucky no other soldiers attacked us, but on those nights when Monier called, I couldn't help but take pride in the approach we'd taken.

Thumos, the lion, is built to protect its own. It loves armor. I'd expected all that to be in full force as a Marine at war. I'd expected a band of brothers. Us against the world. But what I'd found instead felt like a band of strangers, misfits, and stepbrothers. The "us" I'd imagined grew larger over time.

When I first learned of *thumos*, the most jarring aspect had been its unabashed strength. Reading the Greeks, I'd felt a new part of me come alive. It was an aggressive part, the part of me that could fight for something. It was the part of me that was willing to die for something.

But with the fierceness of the lion comes also the ability to make friends, to give one's heart. That aspect had always been confusing to me. One of my professors once wrote a piece in our college magazine, disturbed by the fact that playful dolphins could also ruthlessly murder. A similar tension shows up in the motto I've already mentioned: "No Better Friend, No Worse Enemy, Than a United States Marine." Yet it's the same power that makes us gentle to friends and fierce to enemies. And it's what puts us on high alert with strangers, who've yet to show whether they're one or the other.

Although naturally wary of the foreign and unfamiliar, *thumos* is nonetheless the part of us that can go to an exotic land and make it home. It's the part of us that can take a stranger and decide, "Here is my friend." The lion is the part of us that holds things dear.

In Afghanistan, I was starting to understand that apparent tension more deeply. As much as I felt that I'd never seen my ambition realized in some glorious moment on the battlefield, it had come alive in more ways than I'd envisioned. Standing at the halfway point of my deployment, I was no longer the same young man intent on exhibiting his strength and valor in battle. I was in a new landscape. The lion was still developing as a character in my story. He didn't have quite the same edge, the same driving aggression, as he did before. But there was even more that I had to discover about him.

PART II RETROSPECTIVE

- To build any large alliance, you'll have to build trust with people you otherwise wouldn't. The farther you get from your team, the less the people are like you (see "Too Many Bullets," page 73; "Snarling at Strangers," page 90).
  - *You'll need to mediate and negotiate boundaries, delineating what's expected from whom.*
  - *You'll need to carve out your own authority and defend fragile legitimacy.*
  - *You'll need to take tangible steps to build trust.*
- Anger is offensive, defensive, and useful.

  - **Offensive:** *Anger is the part of us that will hold people accountable for betrayal, incompetence, negligence, unreliability, and deception (see "Too Many Bullets," page 73; "Snarling at Strangers," page 90).*
  - **Defensive:** *It's the part of us that protects the things we love, defends boundaries, and stands loyal against all apparent reason (see "Too Many Bullets," page 73; "Snarling at Strangers," page 90).*
  - **Useful:** *When something you love is attacked, you're supposed to get angry. Anger pushes you when calculation tries to hold you back.*

- All power worth having is political. Legitimacy is negotiated. It's always a matter of acknowledgment and consent (see "The Hierarchy," page 76; "Unruly Jades," page 87; "Snarling at Strangers," page 90; "Absolute Power," page 102; "King of Griefs," page 112).
- Socrates's hydra-lion-human is parliamentary: It's not a hierarchy of mind over everything else. Each has a voice and deserves a hearing (see "The Hierarchy," page 76; "Unruly Jades," page 87). These three parts have checks and balances. Anger, the lion, ensures that the hydra cannot slither free. Anger also ensures that the rational mind doesn't become a tyrant.
- Disagreement, conflict, and negation are indispensable tools in sorting out what you most want to be. Boundaries need to be broken all the time if there's going to be an expansion of the self (see "Playing with Boundaries," page 81).
- Negotiations aren't merely transactional or coercive. They're

a sort of dance, one that requires your responsiveness (see "Fruit by the Foot," page 79; "Playing with Boundaries," page 81; "Snarling at Strangers," page 90).

- Authority comes from what the people around you will allow you to do (see "Playing with Boundaries," page 81; "Snarling at Strangers," page 90; "King of Griefs," page 112; "Not a War Story," page 3).

  – *When authority is simply bestowed, it's weak and precarious (see "Unruly Jades," page 87; "Absolute Power," page 102; "King of Griefs," page 112; "Rank Is Nothing," page 129).*
  – *If we test boundaries and get away with it, we expand our authority by getting new permission (see "Playing with Boundaries," page 81; "Unruly Jades," page 87; "Absolute Power," page 102; "King of Griefs," page 112).*
  – *When we get away with transgressing the same boundary over and over, we enlarge our authority (see "King of Griefs," page 112).*
  – *Being right has an authority all its own (see "Not a War Story," page 3).*

- Anger doesn't need to be rigid. It can be made responsive to circumstances, navigating the politics. It should often work through diplomacy (see "Armored Off," page 85; "Snarling at Strangers," page 90; "King of Griefs," page 112).
- Anger is what pushes back when a boundary is transgressed. It's the policing power of authority (see "Snarling at Strangers," page 90; "Navigating the Gray," page 99; "King of Griefs," page 112).

- In a position of command, it's easy to think you can dispense with mediation, that you can take obedience for granted. You never can (see "Unruly Jades," page 87; "Absolute Power," page 102).
- Building trust is more tangible than you might think. It's not a spiritual mandate; there are mechanisms involved, upkeep (see "A Goat in Sheep's Clothing," page 93; "Gifts and Gratitude," page 97; "Invisible Armor," page 114).
    - *Giving and accepting gifts graciously can build your relationships. People are angry when their offers are refused (see "A Goat in Sheep's Clothing," page 93; "Gifts and Gratitude," page 97).*
    - *Loyalty is built standing by a friend when it's not convenient (see "Turning Them into Us," page 104).*
    - *Hear both sides of a story. Give the benefit of the doubt. You can't form an alliance if you demonize strangers (see "The Permanent Difficulty of Translation," page 107; "Inside Jokes," page 109).*
- Being nice—even compassionate or kind—isn't enough to become a faithful ally. Loyalty takes strength, sometimes even guile (see "Inside Jokes," page 109).
- Being a loner—excellent and independent—may look attractive, but it's limited. An ensemble can play more music than a solo act. The more beautiful life requires other characters in your story (see "Chimpanzee Politics," page 51; "Machine Guns Up," page 56; "Benevolent Tyranny," page 60; "Winning the Wrong Game," page 63; "You'll Never Go to War," page 67).

    - *How do you know it's more beautiful?*
        - When you drag your team to excellence, it's often humiliating and shameful. Shame tells you when you're ugly (see "Chimpanzee Politics," page 51; "Benevolent Tyranny," page 60; "Winning the Wrong Game," page 63).
        - You might be surprised how satisfying it is for respect to go both ways (see "Machine Guns Up," page 56).
        - When you're treated like the dead weight, it's obvious that the story is limited (see "You'll Never Go to War," page 67).
- You'll almost never have enough power on your own. Coalition and cooperation are indispensable tools (see "Chimpanzee Politics," page 51).
- You'll be shocked at the things people will do for you when you make their effort minimal. Make yourself easy to help (see "You'll Never Go to War," page 67).
- It's easy to look at your team as people you need to drag across the finish line. But excellence requires more care, even for dead weight (see "Chimpanzee Politics," page 51; "Moses's People," page 54).
- The instinct to protect your team is a path to caring for them and becoming one of them. "We" > "I" (see "Moses's People," page 54; "Machine Guns Up," page 56).
- People aren't pawns (see "Benevolent Tyranny," page 60).
    - *When you treat them like that, you shortchange your own glory and your satisfaction is hollow (see "Benevolent Tyranny," page 60; "You'll Never Go to War," page 67).*

  - *When you allow yourself to be treated as a pawn, you'll likely end up treating your subordinates as pawns too (see "Winning the Wrong Game," page 63).*

- You should be ready to choose the mission over your men, but the better default is your men over the mission (see "Winning the Wrong Game," page 63).
- It's noble to accept consequences, but in real life, the mind still needs to step in to escape them sometimes (see "You'll Never Go to War," page 67).

Part III

CYNICISM AND COHERENCE

Chapter 6

NOT THE USUAL SUSPECTS

When I'd started in the Marines, I thought that the hydra was the obvious culprit for most of my problems. He was the reason I slept in too late, skipped workouts, and ate too much.

The small man, my mind, seemed like the only one who might be able to control my hydra. To me at the time, this was the obvious struggle in life—the small man was all-knowing but weak; the hydra was wild and unpredictable but strong.

I figured I could solve their imbalance by putting the small man in charge and making the lion his enforcer. The small man would know exactly what to do and the lion would just carry out orders. They'd be like a judge and his bailiff, a mob boss and his henchman. But just as I'd come to see there was more than met the eye in the lion, I'd started to grow more suspicious of the small man as well. My mind was more of a problem than I'd ever imagined.

It turns out that the lion isn't the small man's pet. He's not simply there to carry out the small man's directives. Sometimes he may be his ally, but his main role is protector of the whole. When the hydra gets out of hand, the lion chases him back; when the mind makes unreasonable demands, the lion threatens a bite. He's not anyone's pawn.

It's easy to think that you should use anger and shame to carry out your small man's wishes. People do that every January with their New Year's resolutions. The mind picks some tyrannical fantasy, and then willpower is expected to carry out that plan for the next 12 months. We fancy ourselves perfect bosses but lazy employees.

But the willpower approach almost always fails because it's a misuse of the lion. The lion isn't there to blindly carry out orders like a robot. He's there to weigh in too. The lion makes sure that things like honor and loyalty are factored in. And just as the lion can be disgusted with the hydra at times, he can also be disgusted by some of the disengaged calculations that the small man is often inclined to make.

It's easy to believe that the small man is our true self, disguised at times by our appetites and our tempers. Even in Socrates's metaphor, he is, in fact, a man, just as we are. But when we allow ourselves to believe that the mind always knows best, that we're deeply rational, that we know the right things to do but simply have a hard time executing on them, the end is predictably hollow.

Many people, believing deeply that reason is a sort of god

on earth, fall victims to cynicism. Of course things don't add up, they say. Talk of gods, heroes, and romance are no more than the crutches weak people need to get through the day. But the mind, they suppose, always knows the truth.

This is the real danger and the hardest to dispel, especially for smart people. Cynicism seems to be the only worldview that has an answer to all contingencies. It's the one full picture of the universe. Our lives don't matter. Anything we build will crumble. When we die, no one really cares.

But this view, tempting as it is for its clarity, isn't the full picture.

DISAPPOINTED AND DISENGAGED

Before ever experiencing a war zone, I'd imagined that such a life-and-death situation would demand all of my attention, that my animal instincts would have me on constant high alert. Yet as our time in Afghanistan drew on, I found that I was in greater danger of merely checking out.

I'd been romantic about the war before I'd arrived, picturing that everything would fit into some larger, more significant whole. On one later occasion, I flew to Kabul for a few days to check out an Afghan Intelligence School we were helping with. Two soldiers from the US Army led our convoy to the school. They were a goofy pair who didn't take themselves too seriously. I remember when I met them, they felt like characters in a new story. Then, on our drive to the school, they were hit with a car bomb and killed. There was no story after all.

Playwrights have a maxim known as Chekhov's gun. It says that if there's a gun hanging on the wall in Act I, then it needs to be fired by the final act. While I was in Afghanistan, I saw many guns on the walls that never did get fired. New characters and initiatives would look like the start of a new chapter, yet they would soon disappear without anyone noticing. I'd have glimpses of our successful adventure playing out, then be quickly convinced that we hadn't moved forward at all.

If we'd progressed, I didn't see it. For all our planning and patrolling, the Afghan soldiers didn't seem much better and the Taliban didn't seem weakened. On the Marine side, I hated my boss, rolled my eyes at my peers, and struggled to lead my subordinates. It was all I could do not to disengage, to start hiding out from my boss and ignoring the Afghans. As far as I could see, there wouldn't have been much difference if I hadn't gone there in the first place.

The big machine was going to keep moving whether I was there or not, and although I loved the Marine Corps, it wasn't going to be loving me back. I was a cog in a broken system, fighting a war that shouldn't have been waged in the first place. Part of me still longed to be a good lieutenant, to be excellent in my role. But another part was tempted to just start counting the days until I was home. Dealing with these thoughts, in myself and in my team, became increasingly critical, if there was to be any hope of doing my job well.

Our team mostly lived off dry cereal, M&M's, and protein powder. But out on patrol, we'd often stop at a Marine base called FOB Geronimo, where they had a full cafeteria that served ice cream. Whenever my Marines heard FOB

Geronimo mentioned in an order, they'd lick their lips. Think training Afghans who might be your enemy is a challenge? Try showing up at FOB Geronimo when the ice cream's gone.

I used to think that betrayal happened in one big break of trust. But often the sense of betrayal comes through an accumulation of much smaller moments. When a marriage ends, people ask what happened, suspecting something acute and dramatic like an affair. But often it's the small promises broken day after day, letting life fall short of expectations, and getting used to disappointment.

Before I became a Marine, it seemed like any trouble I had as a Marine would be instantly serious, that any suffering in Afghanistan would be noble. People often think the same way about entering a marriage or starting a new job, as though the context imbues their actions with meaning. But after a while, the spouse, the company, and the adventure lose their novelty. Disenchantment arrives one little letdown at a time.

Every day it seemed to get clearer that things would never add up. There was no secret meaning, no deeper wisdom, no grand scene in which our lives would come into harmony and significance. We felt like unimportant characters in a story no one cared to hear.

RANK IS NOTHING

Block—a fellow lieutenant—was 6'3", beefy, and always looked lost and ready to fight. He couldn't stand to hear me talk about our team. "LeBlanc," he'd say, "Do me a favor and stop fucking pretending like we do anything here. That's fine when you're talking to the Marines, but seriously."

To Block, there was nothing worth dying for in this war. There might not be anything worth dying for anywhere. To him, the trash piles surrounding the camp, the fact that most of the Afghans had never touched a computer, and the lack of working plumbing made it all completely hopeless. Perhaps there was honor in the last war. Maybe Iraq had honor. Korea must have. But not here. Not with these smells; not with these people.

One day, as I was cleaning guns, Block walked up twirling the keys to the pickup around his finger. He'd been out to Camp Dwyer, the main Marine position, which was only a short drive away. When remote teams came in, they'd go there to get haircuts and do laundry.

"What's up, dude?!" Block called to me. He opened a bag of popcorn and popped a piece in his mouth. "We just ditched Tugger."

"Yeah," I said, half listening. Block was a lieutenant; leaving a captain without a ride back to base would be a serious charge, even if it was just Tugger.

Captain Tugger was a well-intentioned officer who'd unfortunately forgotten that the Marines had anything to do with war. We used to speculate that Captain Schueman's ancestors might have been cobblers, and we likewise wondered what a long line of Tuggers might be known for.

There's always a tension between rank and talent in the Marine Corps, as there has been in all armies going back to Achilles and Agamemnon. When better maturity and judgment correspond with increasing rank, it's amazing how strong and effective the hierarchy can be. But all it takes is a very talented lance corporal or an incompetent captain to cast a serious shadow over the structure, and what used to be respect gets reduced to jewelry on collars. Captain Tugger was the kind of captain who threatened the best meaning of rank.

I'd assumed that Block was overstating it when he said he'd ditched Tugger, at least until I later saw Captain Tugger walking up to us, fuming. We were sitting on the porch. Block said loudly, "There he is! I thought we lost this guy on Dwyer."

I laughed.

"You left me at Camp Dwyer!" Tugger yelled furiously. Block hadn't embellished at all. Ditching a captain on a different base wasn't dangerous, but it was wildly disrespectful. Block's lion, the part that would care about such things, was absent.

Block played dumb. "Where did you go, sir?"

"To get a haircut!" Tugger replied, still yelling. "I told you I was going to get a haircut. And you left me!" Amazingly enough, Block remained relaxed in his chair, without tensing at all.

"O—kay," he said, dripping with condescension, as if Tugger were freaking out over nothing. "Well, that explains it, sir."

"What the fuck 'that explains it'!" Tugger screamed, losing his temper and bearing. Although I knew that Tugger was in the right, his shrieking tone, in contrast with Block's studied calm, suggested otherwise. "I told you where I was and you fucking left me!"

"Hey, sir," Block said, putting his hands up in pseudo surrender. "Don't get angry with me. I'm a victim." Playfulness could be a form of aggression. Block had it mastered.

"What the fuck?" Tugger couldn't believe his ears.

"I'm a victim here," Block explained. "Those other guys told me you went to a beauty salon. I said, 'That's not funny. Captain Tugger's all man. He doesn't go to beauty salons.'" In Block's astonishing reconstruction, he'd managed to recast his own aggression as victimhood. It was a sight to see.

"The barbershop was called a beauty salon!" Tugger yelled. He got his composure and tried a new line: "But you went to Dwyer with four and you left with three! Why didn't you look for me if you didn't believe them!"

"I didn't know what to believe, sir," Block said. He began to wrap things up. "Glad it all worked out in the end, though."

"Block," Tugger said, reasoning with him, "I'm a fucking captain."

"I'm pissed off, too, sir. I get it," Block said, ignoring the weight of Tugger's statement. "We're the victims here. I'm just glad you got back okay." Captain Tugger was dumbfounded. "I hate to cut us short, sir," Block concluded as he stood up. "But these guys need the key, so I've got to run it over to them."

With that, he jogged away to return the truck key to no one. Tugger stood there in shock for a moment, collected himself, and walked inside the tent. Block never got any kind of punishment for leaving a captain behind. My guess is that it was too embarrassing for Tugger to report to anyone.

Block had come out on top in the exchange, but it wasn't

a victory. Rather than winning or losing, he'd refused to play the game. What he thought of as being above rank actually just took him out of the ranks. He left our tour without patrolling much or seeing much of anything. When we returned to the States, he immediately put in his papers to leave the Marines.

Tragedy often happens around characters who won't accept the role they're given. Hamlet couldn't get himself to play the avenger. Lear could no longer play king and father together, nor could Regan and Goneril play his daughters for longer than a scene. Block couldn't get himself to play the role of the dutiful subordinate.

I saw this in my kids when they were in kindergarten. At home, they'd be funny and interesting. But when asked to play the role of student, peer, or friend, they were uncomfortable and shy. They had to learn how to bring themselves into the role.

When I started my first robotics company, I came to see just how common this problem is in adults. Young people especially come into their careers confused about how to fit in. Some can't help but to turn into sycophants and yes men. They can't find the right way to bring themselves to the role. Others refuse the role of subordinate and can't treat their boss with any respect. They seem to think that the choice is between a naive belief in hierarchy or a dismissive cynicism about it. They leave out the possibility of putting on a sort of play together, where the ranks or positions are indicative but not immovable.

That sort of sophisticated play needs a sense of humor and optimism to work. The grown man who still texts his mom he got home safe or the husband who eats the vegetables his wife insists on both understand the play. In the wrong mood, the roles can feel insulting. But both wife and mother want what's best for the man. Letting them play their roles brings out the best in the scene.

ALL THE WORLD'S A STAGE

One of Shakespeare's most famous lines comes from one of his least known characters. "All the world's a stage, and all the men and women in it merely players," is spoken by a character named Jaques. In his view, nothing in human life is too real or serious. All of what we see amounts to acting on the parts of the people involved.

All of what we see is simply acting. In the context of the play, Jaques is disgusted by ordinary humans, by their lies, dressing up, and posturing. He forsakes life in the king's court to go live in the woods. It's there that he casts his famous judgment that people are merely actors.

Jaques's famous line is followed by a dark summation of human life. His Seven Ages of Man speech (as it's often called) runs through a series of recognizable moments that the listener naturally expects to come together like puzzle pieces, forming a coherent and beautiful picture. But instead of revealing life as a pilgrimage, or a growth in wisdom, Jaques presents a collection of disjointed snapshots that don't add up. This is what the analytic mind, the small man, often risks: dissecting the parts until there's no whole left.

Following birth, Jaques says that man grows from a

puking baby to a whining schoolboy; in love, he writes bad poetry about his girlfriend's eyebrow; becoming a man, he tries to prove how tough he is in war; he comes back without honor and takes a corrupt job to get rich; finally, he loses his voice and strength before sinking into mere oblivion. It's a depressing picture of life, but not an unfamiliar one.

In a certain mood, parents will talk about their babies as crying machines in constant need of diapers. Almost everyone has an embarrassing story about a ridiculous poem or song they wrote when they were in love. Young men will forever be beating their chests, while bureaucrats and public servants will always skim a little off the top. Anyone who's seen old age up close knows it isn't pretty. There's a natural fear that through all these stages nothing will connect and there won't be a proper ending.

Yet, while people do act, and Jaques's stages of life have been easily recognized by all, the "merely" is where his wisdom breaks down. People are actors, but that's not all they are. As Shakespeare shows throughout the rest of the play, almost all of the characters play different roles, often several at once. They even wear disguises and change their names.

But beneath the dressing up, there are coherent, even lovable souls. Although the thought that "all the world's a stage" is often attributed to Shakespeare, as the playwright he undercuts his character's speech almost immediately. Directly after Jaques's famous declaration, Shakespeare portrays strangers becoming friends, characters treating one another with great generosity and consideration, and an old man coming onstage supported by the grateful young man he'd helped raise.

Missing from Jaques's bleak account are the parents who adore their babies and make so many sacrifices on their behalf. Missing, too, are the brothers and sisters they share the world with. He skips the curiosity of children, their education, and the friendships they form. He doesn't mention that love often turns into marriage, and marriage into a family. Jaques either doesn't see or chooses not to notice the leadership, loyalty, service, or sacrifice of soldiers. And even his grim picture of the man on his deathbed misses the people that may be at his bedside: his wife, his friends, his children, perhaps even his priest.

When my aunt was in the hospital, unable to speak or move during her final days, my cousin rushed to her hospital room with his newborn son so that my aunt could meet her first grandchild. It was unlikely she had any way of sensing that the baby was there. Yet when she died the following day, everyone agreed that she'd somehow been waiting for that moment. It was heart-wrenching and sad, but far from what Jaques called mere oblivion.

Connections are always richer than Jaques pictured. My dad has an old Afghan guitar hanging on his wall that looks like a piece of quirky furniture. Both Afghan customs departments and US customs ensure that wood can't transfer from country to country, yet I smuggled that guitar from a small market in Marjah all the way to our small Ohio town. We're not a family that has many trophies up, but my dad loves that guitar. To him, it doesn't just represent the year his son spent in a combat zone, but stands for the playful labor I still had in me at the end of it. Even exhausted from hundreds of patrols and feeling the weight of US policy decisions on my back, I thought to buy a funny-looking guitar to bring home to my dad.

I got several awards for my time in Afghanistan, but the one that makes me happiest is that silly guitar on my dad's wall. The small man would dismiss such stories. After all, what's special about an old guitar from a third world country? But the lion knows better. People aren't "merely" anything.

WITH FRIENDS LIKE THESE

It's easier to think of the mind as the parent and the appetites as the child. The hydra whines for instantaneous pleasures and the mind wisely counsels against them. But I was now starting to see that the analytic edge of the mind came with its own dangers. I thought back to a time in my training when I'd seen some of my smarter peers letting their minds cause them trouble. Reflecting on the story, I started to see that fellowship was more than a blind spot for the mind; it could be an antidote.

Lieutenant Martin was a buddy of mine who was thoughtful and articulate. A few weeks into an infantry training course, he couldn't help calling out how ridiculous the training scenarios were.

"Why are we training without warming layers?" he'd ask anyone listening, "If we were good infantry officers, wouldn't we have checked a weather report?" Martin's take on things was attractive. On his better days, he seemed like the cool stand-up comedian, calmly above the absurdities he observed.

This is how the small man of the mind works: Cynicism reinforces his sense of autonomy. He likes being aloof, looking down on the lion and hydra as wild beasts. Martin's commentary earned him a small following of other Marines, a sort of club of murmurers. Soon, though, Martin decided to drop out of the course and it wasn't long before the others followed. Once they'd put the small man absolutely in charge, they couldn't quite engage again.

My Grandpa Art would always say, "play with a dirty stick and you're going to get dirty." It's a tough lesson because it feels like we can play as much as we want, so long as we avoid the dirty part. When my first business was starting to grow, I spent a lot of time with other guys leading companies. Parts of them were great. They had interesting ideas and taught me a lot about business. But they also loved getting drunk and a few of them could get sleazy away from their wives.

I wanted to think that I could simply engage with the business parts of them, just as Martin's buddies thought they could laugh off his comments. But people are more like stews than salads. It's hard to separate out one part without taking on their whole logic. I wasn't just learning about hiring practices, I was learning their world view. And that world view included permission for some things I didn't want. The only answer was to stop spending time with them altogether.

Fortunately, it also works the other way too. When I'm working on being a better husband, I try to spend more time with people in happy marriages. When I want to get in better shape, I hang out with friends who work out. It's a very simple action that helps deal with some seemingly unsurmountable problems. The mind, of course, tends to reject this solution, relying instead on analyzing the problem and trying to find specific fixes.

This issue became clear to me when I decided to go to business school after the Marines. Most people take on that challenge analytically, focusing solely on the GMAT. I took a different approach. I sought out as many people as I could from the top 10 business schools and asked them all about how they studied and filled out their applications. After I'd talked to dozens of them, I knew what good essays were, how I should position myself, and how to study effectively for the GMAT. The analytic approach fell short of the fellowship approach.

RIGHT OR MARRIED?

There's a saying that bothered me for years: Do you want to be right, or be married? All husbands and wives know this feeling. The perfect snarky response comes to mind. They know it will get them in trouble, but they can't help but show how smart, superior, and quick they are.

The aphorism sounds like a surrender. It seems like it's suggesting you should agree with something that's wrong so that your spouse doesn't get mad at you. But there's a lot more to it. Before I was married, I learned this lesson about misplaced cleverness in Afghanistan (though that hasn't stopped me from repeating it).

Captain Shinn had gotten word that our regimental commander would be visiting our base the next day. He told me to prepare a brief about enemy trends in our area.

I was excited. After operating for months in our area, I knew Southern Helmand better than my hometown. My Marines and I had patrolled the area just about every day, and I'd drunk hundreds of cups of chai as I met with leaders and locals in my effort to understand our space. I knew the good routes from the bad ones and the safe corners from the threats. Still, this was the regimental commander, and I wanted to be ready with more.

So I stayed up most of the night learning more. I studied all the intelligence reports I could, trying to understand the connections between all the Taliban leaders. I read everything I found about Taliban funding in the area and how they were working to expand their influence.

When Shinn walked in the next morning, I was exhausted and proud of myself. I had a cup of room-temperature coffee in my hand and a wall filled with sticky notes spelling out the Taliban network. I'd learned names I could barely pronounce yet couldn't wait to say them out loud.

But when the regimental commander arrived, we didn't go to our tent for a briefing. Instead, he wanted to meet immediately with the Afghan Army commanders. So we sat for a few hours with them, drinking more chai and having a general discussion about the region and its issues.

As we walked back to our corner of the base, the commander turned to me. "Are you all safe operating around here?" he asked. "We've been seeing an uptick in IEDs. Is that from increased enemy activity? Or are we just hitting a bunch of old ones?"

The question felt too simple to me. Our safety hardly depended on whether the IEDs were old or not. I thought he really needed to grasp how the enemy leaders were working together. "Sir," I began, "to understand our current threat, you need to understand the dynamics that Taliban commanders are facing."

I carried on about the enemy networks, regurgitating everything I could remember from the night before. I proudly rattled off names I imagined no other lieutenant would know.

"So, it's increased enemy activity?" my commander asked, confused.

"It's about the leaders, sir," I began, preparing to correct him.

Shinn broke in. "Sir, we don't believe there's increased enemy activity. Those new IED hits are coming from the drug task force that's been following a bunch of routes that haven't been driven in years." Shinn and Treglia did all the talking the rest of the way back, without the commander consulting me any further.

A little while after he left, I was discussing our meeting with the other lieutenants. "He asked me a question but my answer went way over his head," I told them with a laugh. At that point, it was just another example of how absurd the war was. Although I was joking, my underlying mood was growing cynical and jaded. The commander couldn't recognize good information when I said it right to his face.

As I was talking with the lieutenants, I didn't notice that Shinn had walked up and overheard me. "You didn't answer his question," he interrupted.

"Sir?"

"Your answer didn't go over his head," he said, prepared

to press his point. "He asked you a simple question and you rambled on about all the names you memorized."

"Sir," I responded, no longer smiling, "I literally stayed up all night learning everything about the enemy. The colonel was asking about IEDs, when what he really needs to know is that the Taliban leadership is in total disarray."

"There are only six things you need to know to brief," he said, ignoring me. "Who, what, when, where, why, and how much will it cost. If you're talking to a decision-maker, those are the six questions you find answers to. You knew those answers before you studied. You stayed up all night just to learn the wrong answer."

"Well, sir, I think that understanding an enemy may be a bit more complicated than the five W's," I said, surprised that Shinn didn't seem to appreciate the nuance.

"The enemy is complicated," Shinn said, "and the colonel knows that even better than you do. But he has big decisions to make fast. He needs to be confident that his lieutenant has taken the details into account and sifted out the information most relevant to his decision. He could read intel reports himself."

Shinn was right and I knew it. It had been easy for me to treat the commander as a cartoon, as though he embodied the soldier's cliché of disconnected brass. But the truth was I'd written him off too soon and very unfairly. I was accurate but irrelevant.

The lesson was simpler than I wanted it to be: I was too damned pleased with myself. That's how it often works with the mind. There we are with soldier's lives or our marriage on the line, and we can't help but showcase how smart and clever we are. Sometimes, the small man just can't help himself.

The colonel had asked about IEDs and my response was that he was worried about the wrong thing. I'd stepped out of what he needed from me, performing instead for an audience that wasn't there.

WATER FROM A ROCK

Reading *The Prince*, Machiavelli's notorious book on the ruthless nature of power, I was surprised to find Moses counted as a prince. Alongside tyrants and mass murderers, the biblical hero is presented as a prime exemplar of Machiavellian statesmanship. But most of my surprise came from the fact that Moses had never struck me as a leader. He seemed to do whatever God told him. When I became a lieutenant, though, I found myself taking a second look.

Moses's story is one of freeing his people from slavery in Egypt and leading them through the desert to the Promised Land. In the earlier stages, God empowers Moses's staff to act as a sort of magic wand. It's featured in several of the famous plagues sent to convince Pharoah he must let the Hebrews go. When they have to get across the Red Sea quickly, because they're being pursued by Pharaoh's soldiers, Moses uses his staff to part the sea so that they can walk through. He's an intermediary leader, God's lieutenant.

As the story unfolds, Moses is comfortable as the medium of divine power, and with each miraculous act, his standing as the leader of the Hebrews increases. Later, though, God commands him to bring forth water from a rock, not with his staff but by speaking to it. Surrounded by his thirsty and starving people, Moses doesn't quite trust that his words will be enough and he strikes the rock twice with his staff. Although he failed to honor in full the task that God had commanded, water sprang forth from the rock nonetheless.

It's a crucial moment. Part of me wondered whether breaking free from slavish adherence to God's commands would be the moment that Moses really became a leader, the moment when he'd finally become his own man. But directly after he relies on the proven power of his staff rather than the new, unknown, and mysterious power of His word, Moses is told that, although he'll be leading his people to the Promised Land, he'll never get to set foot there himself. Moses had in fact failed the final test. He hadn't seen the subtler, more spiritual thing that God had wanted him to do.

Moses was unable to fully trust invisible powers to act on the world. Nervous in front of his people, he couldn't help but engage the world they all can see, while ignoring the voice that he alone can. We all know the impotence he feared. It's the way we feel whenever we tell someone to do something and they don't do it. We feel it when we command a dog to come and it doesn't or we tell a kid to stop and he keeps on running.

All commands are invisible power. We lock our doors at night when we don't trust the invisible power of the law. We put our dog on a leash if we don't trust that he'll come when we call. We get nervous before a confrontation at work where we'll be telling someone they need to do something different. What if they don't listen?

But when we relegate our authority to only the things we can physically control, we limit our ability to operate and be effective. There's only so much we can build when we can't establish a spiritual authority.

When the small man of the mind stops believing in the meaning of things he can't see, he resorts to force. He doesn't trust in matters of honor, loyalty, duty, reverence, and wonder. He can only play in the physical world, not the moral one. He can be clever, but he can't be wise. This is always the risk of the mind when it's alienated, when it's allowed to run freely over the lion. But when the lion engages, new possibilities emerge.

Chapter 7

OWN THE MESS

ONE DAMN THING AFTER ANOTHER

During my time in Afghanistan, I led patrols for thousands of miles in a combat zone. Almost daily, I was briefing my team on where we'd be going and why. I spent my mornings making sure we had enough ammunition, food, and water. I crawled in the back of our trucks to check our radios and communication jammers. I checked the young Marines' pockets to make sure they had tourniquets.

I expected that those operations would be where I learned the most. I thought those stories would be the ones I'd tell my kids someday. Instead, when I think of Afghanistan, I think about the Afghan Intelligence Officer who rubbed his feet and offered me grapes.

The reason is that our patrols were mostly akin to driving

through Texas. Long bouts of desert without much happening. Sure, we'd occasionally hit an IED, get a few shots in our bulletproof glass, or pick up a few detainees. One time, we stayed up for 72 hours in search of a sniper team that had stopped communicating with headquarters. But it would be a stretch for me to call any of it meaningful.

Sometimes my kids ask to hear stories about our patrols and I can barely find enough of an arc to make it sound like an anecdote. We'd drive for hours, the Afghans might get hurt or need something, and we'd drive back. Most of the days didn't turn into stories with a beginning, a middle, and an end. They were messy and boring. But that's mostly what reality is: a mess.

A lot of adults I know stop there. Reality is meaningless. We live and we die. One damn thing after another. For many people, raising their kids becomes the one obviously meaningful thing they do, while the rest turns into a slog in service of them. The commute, the boss who just doesn't understand, the corporate hoops to jump through, the long line at the grocery store—those experiences make up a major chunk of our time. So we turn our brains off during those times. For the most part, we disengage.

Then later, we make up for the lost time by seeking easy pleasures. We enslave the small man to bean counting during the day and let our hydra run wild at night. Our lion is mostly kept in his cage. If honor is suggested by someone at work, it's usually dismissed as naivete or explained away in merely economic terms. No one expects that we care about trust or honor, unless it affects the bottom line. The one domain where there's still deep care is in physical safety. We've all wisely been able to agree that most of what we do isn't worth anyone losing their lives for.

I was torn between my idealistic hopes for what war might be like and the mundane reality of it. Still, I was learning where my lion had a place in our operations. With growing cynicism, my lion had developed even more, getting me to engage in the sort of play we were all putting on together. Next I had to learn that one of the lion's most important tasks was to take ownership of the mess.

CALLSIGN PRIME

One thing pushing me toward a cynic's view was having a boss who hated me. Major Thorne had taken a special interest in leading me and the other lieutenants, but he didn't offer much in the way of vision or inspiration. It was easy for me to start blaming him for my problems and to rationalize that I would have been good in Afghanistan if I'd had a better leader.

There are some people who are by nature rude, inconsiderate, and hard to be with. Thorne, in contrast, chose to be those things. With people outside our team, he was a different person. He'd let everyone else call him by his callsign, Prime.

Prime was funny, interesting, and capable of strong rapport. Sometimes I'd try to be friendly with him when he was in those moods. Yet no matter how freely he'd been laughing before I approached, the smile would vanish from his face as he turned to me with dead eyes and a look of annoyance: "What do you want, fuck stick?"

"LeBlaaaaanc," Thorne frantically screamed one day. I immediately ran to him, wondering why he hadn't used his radio. He was gazing off into the distance with his sunglasses on.

"Yes, sir?" I responded, out of breath, as I looked all around for the emergency or disaster that might have caused him to scream my name.

"What were you doing?" he said tonelessly, still not even looking at me.

"I was preparing the weapons for patrol," I said.

He continued gazing off into the distance for a moment, then said, still without intonation, "Get the fuck away from me."

I'd dreamed of reporting to someone who would teach me and mentor me as a leader. But unless Thorne was some kind of cursing Zen master, it seemed like he really just despised us.

The lieutenants all made different attempts to appease him. Lieutenant Chevy and I tried to be model lieutenants, but our attempts to connect only resulted in abuse and embarrassment. Lieutenant Block tried sarcasm, which saddled him with some formal penalties that hurt his career. Lieutenant Turner tried reasoning with Thorne, but got open mockery and public humiliation in return. Lieutenant Haberer, a former D-1 athlete who didn't need to say much, tried ignoring him. That seemed to work fairly well, but when I spoke to Haberer about our situation I found that he hated

Thorne even more intensely than I did. And Haberer didn't throw hate around lightly.

With so much focus on our fight with Thorne, none of us were focused on the mission of advising the Afghans. Instead, we all harbored personal grudges, longed for revenge, and couldn't act as one. Frustrated, I went to Captain Shinn to get some advice.

"Do you know how Major Thorne got his callsign?" Shinn asked. Marine pilot callsigns are given in what's called Kangaroo Court, where all the pilots get drunk together and propose names for one another. Typically, they derive from something embarrassing, but I'd never stopped to wonder how Thorne had gotten the nickname "Prime."

"It stands for 'Person Responsible for Instructing Most Everyone,'" Shinn continued. "He's prideful. He can be arrogant. But he's not simply abusing you all. He's trying to get you all to band together. Major Thorne came from a part of the Marine Corps where lieutenants are initiated through being treated harshly. He'll only trust you if he knows you can take it. He wants the lieutenants to join together to stand up to him. Show some confidence and competence."

After I felt so personally wronged and robbed, Shinn helped me see that I'd been too self-involved to see the bigger story. To Thorne, the lieutenants looked like whiny benchwarmers. He wanted confident athletes who were eager to prove themselves. He wanted lieutenants who could bite back with respectful wit when they were insulted. He wanted to see a team of lieutenants determined to earn their authority. When I shared Shinn's insights with the other lieutenants, that's exactly what we did.

Thorne saw his plan working. He wasn't the only one who noticed. The whole team recognized that the lieutenants were stronger and more serious. Thorne and I started to work together almost every day. And once I got to see Prime in action, it was sobering to realize just how much I had to learn from him.

Once we started playing competent lieutenants to get Thorne off our backs, we actually started to become competent lieutenants. We didn't know it at the time, but the older, more experienced Marines we outranked were our audience. They weren't the sort of men who'd ever bow down before a junior officer, but we earned their respect.

Acting like the good lieutenant, I learned a lesson I'd keep with me decades after: Play your role with enthusiasm. When he was envoy to France, Ben Franklin would wear a coonskin cap, playing up an American reputation for being pioneers. Teddy Roosevelt, playing a great, rugged president, got shot but still carried on and finished his speech. Winston Churchill, bleary-eyed and with the butt of a cigar in his mouth, looked like a stubborn old mule who would never surrender.

Thumos is what enables us to play our roles with gusto. These men didn't just mimic their characters; they owned and embodied them. Franklin could have visited France as a proper European negotiator—powdered wig, silk coat, and ready for court. Instead, he embraced all that it was to be an American. Far from shrinking from the role, he demanded its recognition. Many comedians swear that the jokes are less important than looking, talking, and acting funny. It's their spirit that engages us.

Audiences everywhere delight in seeing an actor happily playing his role. No one is engaged when the actors look like they don't even want to be onstage.

LEADERSHIP CHALLENGES

When Staff Sergeant Williams joined our advisor team, he had more combat experience than most of our members. On our second day in Afghanistan, he was in the gunner's turret when his vehicle hit an IED. After a concussion and two nights in medical, he was back, running his mouth and talking his usual trash.

In dealing with enlisted Marines of lower rank, Williams set aside professional obligation and vacillated between treating them as peers or as servants. To senior officers with greater combat experience, he projected the attitude of an up-and-coming star in relation to old legends: Move on, old-timer; it's my stage now. He talked to the lieutenants as though they were schoolkids on a field trip. His example encouraged the senior enlisted Marines to disengage completely.

Despite all of Williams's trash talk, apparent disrespect, and refusal to play the game within the Marine hierarchy, he was a generous teacher. Incompetence was a capital crime, no matter the perpetrator's rank. He was willing to patiently teach the basics to anyone on the team, even after he'd been patrolling all day. Williams was a mess.

I went to Captain Shinn for advice. He was impossible to deal with but far too valuable to get rid of. So instead of trying to work with him, I'd let him railroad me. Rather than challenging him, I'd just let him do what he wanted. I felt like the embarrassed parent of a kid throwing a tantrum.

Shinn's answer to the Williams problem was different: competence. It was the same sort of guidance he'd given me with Thorne. If I wanted authority I could use, I had to earn it by being the most prepared. Williams had the experience, the skills, and the better knowledge. Still, I could know the details of an operation better if I was willing to put in the work.

The perfect opportunity came to put my plan in motion when I was put in charge of a working group to build our defense with the senior enlisted Marines. Since we were living with the Afghans on a corner of their base, it was a sensitive task. We needed enough weapons to defend ourselves but couldn't show the Afghans that we considered them a threat. I chose Williams as my deputy.

I pulled up all my training notes and manuals and studied them hard. I took a careful inventory of the team's available weapons. I ran my plan by Captain Shinn, to check on any special considerations there might be in dealing with a threat from the Afghan Army. I was no expert, but I was prepared.

The meeting assembled and I walked everyone through my plan on our map. Williams wasn't listening. He stared at my proposed positions as though he were watching someone punch themselves in the face, patiently deciding how to tell them they were crazy.

"Uh, sir," he began in thick condescension. "You might want to rethink your weapon placement." He was reacting to the fact that there were no weapons facing the Afghans whose base we shared. He'd paid no attention to what I'd said about that, but I needed to make my correction pointed.

"What in particular, Staff Sergeant?" I replied, baiting him.

"Hmm. I don't know, *sir*," he said, making each word sound more ironic than the last. "Did you ever consider that our biggest threat may not come from the Taliban attacking us from the open desert? I don't want to sound crazy," he continued with complete sarcasm, "but I think our Afghan partners attacking us might be our biggest threat."

Williams's performance raised no smiles or chuckles from the senior Marines. It was a scene they'd watched too many times: the boot lieutenant who's officially in charge gets humiliated by the mouthy staff sergeant. They just rolled their eyes, at both Williams's insubordination and my incompetence.

"And yet," I countered, helping him dig his hole deeper, "aiming machine guns directly at our partners might make it harder for them to trust us."

"Hmm," Williams mocked. "We can either live through this deployment with unhappy partners, or we can die knowing that we're building trust with them. Tough call."

Williams had set himself up for the fall, and I stepped in to deliver the final punch. "How won't the trucks fix that?" I asked. He hadn't listened to the plan and had missed the most important part. "Like I said, the Afghans won't see any weapons from our watch positions because we'll stage trucks with mounted machine guns behind the tents." Everyone was paying attention now. "That'll maintain trust with the Afghans, yet we'll also be able to respond with any needed defense in under a minute."

It was what Shinn and I had worked out. Knowing the details gave me authority, but I was careful not to overplay my hand. Williams took his correction gracefully. "Makes sense, sir," he said without sarcasm. I opened the plan up for discussion. The senior Marines, having watched me finally stand up to Williams, took the planning seriously. For the rest of the meeting, Williams was neither sullen nor hostile. In fact, he was very helpful, free with good suggestions and well engaged in our task.

Not engaging with Williams was like looking at a messy room and not knowing where to begin. It was easier to just accept that the place was trashed and to wish for a cleaner place to live. But Shinn had shown me how I could start by getting the couch immaculate. The defensive planning didn't cure everything with Williams, but it was a clear start.

BEYOND BOSSES

When I decided that Thorne was a bad boss, my inclination was to shut down and disengage. When I saw how insubordinate and crazy Williams was, I tended to back off and work on damage control. In both cases, though, Shinn had other, better guidance for me. Leading as a lieutenant carried with it responsibilities that went both up and down; the answer wasn't to exit, but to muddle through, to wrestle with all the messy realities. The cases of both Williams and Thorne felt unique at the time, but I've since come to appreciate that they belong to a larger, common pattern.

As I started to grasp the deeper continuities in my dealings with Thorne, who was my superior, and Williams, my subordinate, it also helped me make sense of something that had bothered me for years. I've never really liked the word *boss.* To me, it sounds like authority without reason, command without negotiation. That's the understanding my dad had in mind when he chose to base his career and livelihood on starting his own company, so that he'd never have to have a boss.

Seeing everyone as either a domineering boss or as a lazy employee made it easy to absolve myself of the mess. They were bossing me around or I was bossing others around. My lion wanted to rage against the tyranny of it all, but my hydra was afraid of the consequences. My small man decided that it was best to keep the status quo and to simply blame everyone else for the mess we were in.

But when I thought outside of the idea of bosses, I realized that I was in fact surrounded by stakeholders. Above and below, they all had investments to be respected and commitments to be taken into account. We all had shortcomings that needed room for forgiveness. I was starting to see beyond bosses toward the full landscape of command.

I gave myself a new mantra: I report to reality. If I do an incredible job but drive my boss crazy, there's not too much he can do to stop me. If I do a terrible job but my boss thinks I'm a really great guy, there's not much he can do to help me. So rather than focus on how my boss feels or how much rapport I have with a subordinate, I focus on what I think is a good job. I'll take their guidance into account, just as I take my wife's goals or my kid's desires into account when I determine what a good job looks like as a husband and father. But overall, I have the final say.

I carried that mentality with me when I founded my first company, Cobalt. In the beginning, we'd put together a board of very impressive and well-known investors. My cofounders tended to think of them as the bosses. But I used to tell them that I didn't report to them. If I was growing the company at an incredible pace, they couldn't get rid of me, no matter how much they found me personally annoying. If I was running the company into the ground, it wouldn't matter that they enjoyed getting a drink with me; they'd have to fire me. The same was true of my customers.

Both Williams and Thorne needed to fight me before they could respect me. Neither would respect a doormat, yet both resented anyone trying to push them around. They'd enter a command relationship only on the condition of reserving their right to resist and object. If I wanted to bring the best out of Williams or Thorne wanted the best out of me, then domination was a dead end.

While Williams was occasionally willing to listen, he never tolerated being second-guessed on the matters he was best at. To his credit, he also understood his own craziness and could only trust a leader ready and able to pull him back when he went too far. Commanding such a man was a delicate balance. I needed to be competent enough that he'd respect me, but not so pushy that he felt subordinated. He'd concede my freedom and consent to my authority so long as we both understood that he could bite hard if I overstepped.

I'd joined the Marines imagining that as an officer I'd

have full autonomy and scope. It was naive, but I expected to satisfy my lion without taking anyone else's into account. To work with other members of my team, though, I had to find a new framework to avoid lion-on-lion battles. People like Thorne and Williams would naturally attack anything they hadn't had a hand in building. But when I stayed focused on being the best, they'd happily join in.

THE COMFORTS OF SLAVERY

Moses navigates a broken world. He's born to slavery in Egypt. He dies just before his people enter the Promised Land. His life and leadership are spent guiding hungry ingrates for decades through a desert.

The desert itself stands for the broken purgatory we all occupy. Whether leaving a job or a relationship, it's easy for us to think that the choice is between slavery and freedom. We can't wait to remove whatever we see as the shackles, imagining that our lives will instantly and irrevocably be made better. As soon as I leave this job, this marriage, this neighborhood, everything will look up. We fall into the trap of thinking that the new situation will cure all our problems.

Reading Exodus, we might think that the Israelites being freed from the tyranny of the Pharoah is the end of the story. Leaving slavery, we imagine a flourishing freedom as the Israelites walk through the parted sea and on into the sunset. Instead, they leave to wander through the desert for 40 years. In most cases, the path from freedom to flourishing is longer than from slavery to freedom.

The bulk of Moses's story is one of wandering an imperfect stage. But for him, the journey itself is nothing compared to the difficult people he must lead. As Moses learns, it takes more than removing a tyrant to turn slaves into free people. Despite being saved from the Pharoah's tyranny, the Israelites miss the comforts of slavery—the freedom from decision-making, the absence of wrestling with serious decisions. As they wander, starving, they rebel against Moses, wishing again for their old, more secure lives.

In anger, Moses yells at God, asking why God has saddled him with these people. He complains that they're not his babies and says they're too heavy for him to carry. He resents them and his position as their intermediary to God.

I saw Moses as an archetype for the stages I was moving through myself. We first encounter the adult Moses as he watches an Egyptian beating on Israelites. Despite not being accepted as one of the Israelites, he kills the Egyptian. When he takes on the mission of leading God's people from Egypt, it was clearly the Israelites against the Egyptians, Us v. Them. He'd found his imperfect allies. As they traveled on, his group grew as they met and dealt with strangers. Now, faced by rebellion again and again, Moses found himself cynical in the face of unworthy partners.

In Afghanistan, I found myself in this same position. My Marines seemed detached from the mission and impossible to deal with. The Afghans were lazy and lied too much for us to build trust. No one wanted to be there, and I didn't want to lead them.

But as I've reflected before, in the final recounting of his story, Moses gave me some hope that there was a way to build despite the challenges. Just before they enter the Promised Land, he speaks to the Israelites about their journey. For the first time, he uses the words *we* and *us*. Before, he'd only spoken of "you" or "Your people." Moses has acted like an unhappy messenger between God and His people. But in his retelling, he casts himself as one of them, as their leader and teacher.

The first story he recounts in his speech is one of the darker moments of their journey, when, on top of Mount Sinai, God had offered to kill all of the people and to give Moses a new group to lead. But that's not how Moses tells it. Instead, he says that in that moment God had told them to keep moving in their journey.

Perhaps his telling is a noble lie, designed to protect the Israelites from a harsh truth. But it could be that, looking back, Moses sees that God's threat was the moment that Moses became one of the people. By giving Moses the power to fulfill his wish to rid himself of the whining ingrates, He pushed Moses to take ownership of them, to make himself one of them. What had sounded like a credible offer to take the stubborn Israelites out of the picture was in fact a push for them to continue forward together.

Moses is a leader on an imperfect journey. The path is harsh, his people are unworthy, his commander pushes him to do more than he feels capable of. He himself won't be allowed to enter the Promised Land he's worked so hard to reach.

And yet, in his final speech, he takes the flawed band to be his own. He speaks of his harsh conversations as inspirational pushes. He helps his people cross from mere freedom to flourishing. Despite his reluctance, the setbacks, and his contemptible people, looking back, Moses sees that he's managed to help build something beautiful.

TRUST AND LOYALTY

The small man looks at a mess and rationalizes that it's all someone else's problem. All of the stuff in the piles is essentially trash. Everything and everyone is a faulty piece of gear. It's all disposable, lightweight, meaningless in itself. It's the lion that can begin to take ownership of the mess by acknowledging that parts of it are worth saving, that there are seeds of promise and redemption. He knows he needs to work to preserve the things worth keeping.

When I'd joined my team to go to Afghanistan, it looked like I'd joined a motley crew. But Lieutenant Colonel Treglia immediately stood out as someone I respected. In his first speech to our team, my commander, he told us, "There's nothing worth dying for in Afghanistan. Mission success is bringing you home to your families." After hearing that story, even my mom trusted Treglia.

I couldn't imagine not loving Treglia. He never played politics, never changed how he acted, and never complained: He was all lion. As a lieutenant colonel, Treglia had been made the operations officer for a regiment, a good job in his career. Sitting down at his first staff meeting, he joked about a bad plan the regiment had recently put out. "Whose terrible idea was that?" he asked, making fun of his new peers. Everyone sat awkwardly until Treglia's new boss spoke.

"That would be mine," he said.

"Okay . . ." Treglia replied. "But you have to admit, sir, that plan really sucked."

Shortly after, Treglia was fired from the first staff job he'd ever had in the Marine Corps and sent on his seventh deployment to lead Afghan advisors.

In Afghanistan, Treglia wasn't the only senior Marine I dealt with. Lieutenant Colonel Harris, who would soon become Colonel Harris, owned the battlespace we operated in. Unlike Treglia, Harris was a career man. He had a sparkling reputation. When I'd arrived and heard about Harris, I hoped that I would cross paths with him. He was the sort of leader I wanted to learn from.

One day, fueling my vehicles in the middle of a patrol, I got my chance. Lieutenant Colonel Harris had heard that I'd checked in and sent someone to get me. I ran to his office, a small wooden shack in the desert, and introduced myself.

"Lieutenant LeBlanc, right?" he said, getting up from his seat to shake my hand. "Thanks for coming in." I could already see why Harris had his reputation. I didn't know another lieutenant colonel who would have been so warm to a lieutenant he didn't know. "You're with the advisor team down on Camp Alamo, right?" he asked.

"Yes, sir," I replied.

"Who do you report to?" he asked.

"Lieutenant Colonel Treglia, sir," I answered.

"Oh, right, right," he said, nonchalantly. "How is old Phil?"

"It's an interesting deployment," I said, not knowing how Harris felt about Treglia.

"I bet he's eating more goat than he could ever hope for." Harris laughed. I suddenly felt like I was being sold something and didn't like it. Lieutenant colonels didn't tend to invite lieutenants they didn't know into their offices to have polite chat.

"I apologize, sir, but I really should get back to my Marines," I said, trying to cut the conversation short. "Is there anything I can do for you before we head out?"

"I've heard good things about you, LeBlanc," Harris said, reengaging the conversation by force. "It's a shame they put you in that billet. This is your first deployment, right?"

"Yes, sir," I replied. It had already been a bit rude to suggest I needed to leave, but I searched for a way to do it again.

"That's too bad," he said. He was fishing now and I knew it. He wanted to pull some reaction out of me. I stayed silent. "Your role should have been a senior captain, someone who's been around a bit, knows what's going on."

"Is there something you'd like to know about what's going on down in Alamo, sir?" I asked, bristling under his suggestion that I didn't know.

"No, no," he said. "I just—I know Phil. I know how he is. It's just too bad that's who you're reporting to during your first deployment, when you don't know anything yet. A good lieutenant like you, you could have an incredible career with the right leadership. And this is the position they put you in. I'd like to help you."

I couldn't believe what I was hearing. This was a clear invitation for me to switch loyalties. A relationship with Harris was the kind of thing that could help make my career. The small man saw an easy calculation. Treglia was part of the mess. We didn't owe him anything. But my lion stepped in instead.

I looked at Harris straight in the eye and replied, "Lieutenant Colonel Treglia is the best leader I could hope for." I immediately wished that I'd found a cooler way to make my point, but it would do. It was the closest I could come to telling him to go to hell. Harris bristled.

Treglia was part of my messy team. So were Williams and Thorne. But there was far more to all three than met the eye. As I got better at navigating our team dynamics, I wasn't succeeding despite my team, but because of how we all worked together. At times, my team made it easy for me to feel cynical, to blame them for everything that was wrong, to think that if I'd just been with better people, I'd be better. But when I'd started to work with them, they started feeling like my team. What started as an imbalanced mess was becoming a strong foundation on which more beautiful things could be built.

PART III
RETROSPECTIVE

- Betrayal doesn't always come in a grand break of trust. People are betrayed by breaking small promises, falling short of expectations, and habitual disappointment (see "Disappointed and Disengaged," page 127).
- Don't mistake irony for wisdom. When you don't play along with ranks and roles, you rob yourself of the larger story (see "Rank Is Nothing," page 129).
- Embrace your costume. Humor and playfulness are virtues when playing your role (see "Rank Is Nothing," page 129).
- Play your role enthusiastically. Think Teddy Roosevelt playing a rugged president or Ben Franklin in a coonskin cap (see "Callsign Prime," page 149).

- It's easy to look down on the other characters. To say, "I'm here for the mission, not the team." But in doing so, you lose your place in the story altogether. You lose the mission too (see "Rank Is Nothing," page 129).
- People aren't "merely" anything. Families, friends, suffering, death are all parts of a full life (see "All the World's a Stage," page 134).
- Families and friends are what give our lives coherence. They keep our lives from becoming a series of disjointed scenes.
- Humor makes absurdity livable. The right jokes can forge camaraderie. The wrong insights become a toxic pit.
- Nothing shuts people up like competence. When you're under attack, master the facts and your plan (see "Leadership Challenges," page 153).
- All command relationships are secondary to actual results. Top performers understand that they only report to reality (see "Beyond Bosses," page 156).
- We often think that our choice is between slavery (the terrible situation now) and freedom (the wonderful future we imagine). Almost always, those two states are separated by a desert that you'll need to wander through, a desert that might even kill you (see "The Comforts of Slavery," page 159).

Part IV

BUILDING IN A BROKEN WORLD

Chapter 8

THE EDUCATION OF A PRINCE

AFTER CYNICISM

Our culture is obsessed with the solo hero. In movies, books, and TV, we tell stories about the hero who trains up, refines his skills, and overcomes the bad guys. At most, we get a sort of team of superheroes working together to defeat the enemy. But this limited look doesn't take into account the full scope of what heroes may need to negotiate.

Actors move to Hollywood from around the world, ready to prove the naysayers wrong. But once they arrive, they find others like them and begin to make some friends. Then they meet strangers with questionable motives: publicists, managers, agents, and critics. They start to say that they're not paid to act, but to promote, becoming cynical about "the business." A few will face that reality and still make movies to inspire a generation.

Investment bankers reveal a similar pattern. In school, they compete against everyone to prove how smart they are. They win a job at a prestigious bank. They're proud to be on that team and try to earn their place there. But they have their strangers too: clients and vendors, market analysts and lawyers. They become cynical. Do any companies actually realize the savings they build into a merger model? But some will rise out of that disillusionment to win massive deals and help drive our economy.

This arc is the same for anyone breaking into their career. Start with aggressive ambition, find a team, expand into the world, and grow cynical under the countervailing pressures. It's a tale as old as human time. I'm sure there was a caveman who aspired to be the best hunter until he met with strange animals, other tribes, and ungrateful gatherers. Knowing how the pattern works is critical to navigating it with any kind of efficiency. But we almost always stop at the cynicism. It's easy to find adults everywhere who accept their cynical view as the realistic one. They believe they've seen through it all. There were never any real kings, just actors with plastic crowns on their heads.

Yet there's a rare group who are able to move through the cynicism. They don't rely on blind optimism or false idealism, but nonetheless find ways to build on their realistic understanding. They don't let their anger at the mess eat away at them, but let it drive them instead. These people don't live in bitterness after losing someone they love, but live in that person's honor. They're the leaders who, facing impossible odds, maintain a brave face and forge a way through.

These are the generals who make the stars on their collar something worth striving for. They're the kings who give crowns their glory. If we can understand how they moved beyond cynicism, how they could build in a world they knew was fractured or broken, we might find ways to join them as happy warriors.

REINTEGRATING THE MIND

Shakespeare's King Henry V, better known as Prince Hal when he's young, is born into a broken world. It's the world that's left after King Richard, the divine king, is unseated by Bolingbroke, Hal's father. Many expect that Hal will someday inherit the throne, but almost no one, including his father, thinks he'll be good at it.

The world left by Bolingbroke is one of violence, misunderstanding, and lies. Hypocrisy and exaggeration are rampant. Rumors are treated as trustworthy news. Born to that world, Hal grows up fast. He spends his time in bars and whorehouses, chasing cheap pleasures while he can get them. It's hard to stay naive living in Vegas.

We know from history that Prince Hal was heavy into partying as a young man but quickly developed into one of England's strongest kings. Shakespeare, over the course of three plays, illustrates what that development might have looked like, how Hal might have gone from a pranking, cynical teenager to a noble, reigning monarch. His story can serve as a guide and education in navigating our own broken worlds.

To show us Hal's education, Shakespeare sets up two poles: Hotspur, a historical knight and son of an Earl who stands for nobility and tragic heroism; and Falstaff, a made-up character who embodies comic self-interest and calculation. To build in a broken world, Hal needs to understand the integrity of both those poles.

Socrates's strange image of mind (small man), anger (lion), and appetites (hydra), helps makes sense of Shakespeare's poles. Hotspur loves to let his lion rule over his appetites and mind. We hear of him in battle, exhausted, happily risking his life. Falstaff, on the other hand, is full of self-serving schemes and happily indulges all his appetites. In tracing Prince Hal's education, Shakespeare will show us not just which parts of the lion are important, but also how reason and appetite should be allowed their say.

My own story started out much like Hotspur's, chasing after the most noble things I could. Back then, I liked thinking about winning great battles, even if it meant getting wounded or even killed. I was very scared of dying when I thought about it closely, but the idea of dying for my country also seemed so noble that part of me thought it was my clearest path to living a good life. It almost seemed easier to die for something than to live for it.

That idea wasn't quite right, yet neither was it a bad starting point. Nobility and integrity make for the best foundation, but I needed to reintegrate my mind if I was going to shape them properly. To do that, I needed to understand more about Falstaff.

Falstaff was what Shakespeare felt Hotspur was missing. He was calculating, unafraid of the part of himself that wanted to run and hide in the face of danger. Falstaff turned cowardice into an art. He could avoid a fight and later brag about his decisive retreat. Falstaff lies behind the worst part of the politician and even some of the good ones. Maybe in a land with a supreme king and noble subjects, genuine knights were possible. But in Bolingbroke's broken world, one needed a bit of Falstaff to get anything done.

IT DOESN'T MAKE SENSE

The small man doesn't look at bodies with much reverence. Helmand Province was the deadliest area in Afghanistan. Our base was a sort of logistics depot for dead bodies. After Afghan soldiers were killed, we'd help to carry them into planes so their bodies could be taken home. The first time I helped carry one, I didn't know what I was picking up. It seemed far too small to be a body. IEDs didn't send souls off gracefully.

For years, I'd looked at bodies as something to shape and prepare, something that could be turned into a tool for whatever I needed. In war, bodies were just meat bags, carrying organs around the battlefield. All it took was a little hole in the bag and the life came leaking out. Every week, it was a new group that had died. It was easy to lose your sense of purpose.

Marines deployed at the time all faced the same inner conflict: Why were Americans dying for a country whose citizens weren't willing to die for it? That largely unspoken question was once brought decisively into light in an exchange between Captains Barker and Shinn.

Captain Barker could easily have been cast as Falstaff. Looking at him, it was clear that his hydra didn't spend much time hungry. Listening to him made clear that his lion didn't have much of a vote. He'd order a cartoon-sized beer whenever he was out, and his booming laugh would be considered unmannerly at a rodeo. Like Falstaff, whose words seeped out of meter like a belly over jeans, Barker's personality could not fit inside the guidelines set for Marine officers.

Captain Barker had been promoted from lieutenant just before our deployment. The other captains on the team were not happy about it. Particularly unhappy was Captain Shinn.

Shinn was the opposite of Barker. His words, like his body, were strong and lean. He kept his mouth shut often, but lieutenants would study his face, hoping to interpret his smiles or furrowed brow. He'd been an infantry platoon commander and company commander in Iraq—billets that had sculpted his character in the unforgiving school of combat. Captain Shinn was the sort of leader the most ambitious Marines dreamed of having.

Armored in his new rank, Captain Barker lounged around our camp while others hustled. One day, his leg draped over the arm of his chair and playing with a nearby radio, Barker yelled to no one in particular. "This ain't even a war," he bellowed over a lip filled with tobacco. "All y'all are running around here like we're gonna do something. Advise the Afghans? These Afghans'll never be soldiers! It just doesn't make sense. They don't give a damn about saving their country. They just want our money. If they had connections at the poppy farms, they'd be selling that. Just Taliban with a different stream of revenue. And all of you run around like you're gonna do something. It just doesn't make sense."

As Barker carried on about the meaningless mission before us, no one had noticed that Captain Shinn was listening. Shinn waited for a break in Barker's rant, which finally came when he paused to spit his tobacco into an empty water bottle.

"Captain Barker," Shinn began with an evil smile, "thank you so much for educating us about the meaning of our work." Everyone was suddenly tuned in. Marines of the same rank didn't often break in public. But Captain Shinn didn't pull out his gun without people dying. This was going to be a show.

"I'd been under the impression that we were here because we had a duty to our country," Shinn continued. "I thought we stood watch and cleaned weapons to set the example for enlisted Marines and to show them that there's no one whose dignity is above protecting the lives of their fellow Marines. But now you've taught me sense." Marines within hearing froze and paid attention. Shinn clearly wasn't interested in debate. "Sense," as it left his mouth, wasn't a word. It was a noose—one that Captain Barker had unknowingly tied.

"No, sir," Barker said, forgetting he was now the same rank as Shinn. "I was just—"

"No, Captain Barker. I understand. I have to admit I was confused when I thought you were shirking your duty, but now I know it just didn't make any sense. I thought you degraded the name of Marine officers because you were lazy and had no discipline, but now I know it's because that didn't make sense either. Now I see that you've fattened yourself out of regulations because it makes sense, embarrassed your rank because it makes sense, haven't contributed anything to this team, all because it's so important that things make sense."

"Sir—"

"I like things that make sense, too, Captain Barker. To me it makes sense for Marine officers to embody the leadership traits of the Marines Corps. It makes sense that we dedicate our lives to serving our Marines; that we protect their lives even if it costs us our own; that we execute our mission to the fullest extent of our abilities, regardless of personal skepticism or likelihood for success. To me it makes sense to work every hour of the day to be worthy of wearing the same uniform as fallen Marines. I guess I was just confused."

And with that, he left. No one spoke. After a few moments, Barker picked up some nearby papers and pretended to read them. The junior enlisted Marines acted as if they'd just watched the knockout punch in a boxing match. Senior Marines kept their bearing and returned to work, quietly shooting each other knowing glances.

Captain Barker hadn't said anything that wasn't on everyone else's mind. While he was full of hyperbole, he wasn't dumb. He'd given the small man a megaphone and he spoke truly. His skepticism about the mission expressed a rational qualm that had seemed all but silenced by duty. The situation was no accident of modern times or peculiar to Captain Barker; this was a staple of human nature. Barker was Homer's Thersites brought to life and dropped in Afghanistan.

Thersites, as Homer recounts it in the *Iliad*, was the ugliest soldier to go to Troy, an impudent loudmouth. Just after the army is told that they'll remain in what seems a meaningless war, Thersites loudly berates the high brass, accusing them of perpetuating the war to make themselves rich. He objects to being treated as a pawn in a personal game, speaking the minds of the troops around him.

Left unchecked, such thoughts dishearten and fragment. They gnaw at soldiers' minds, drain morale, and form an alliance between the survival instinct of the hydra and the calculation of the mind. *It's a trap!* the small man of the mind screams. *We've been put here to die for no good reason. Don't walk into the trap. Protect yourself, just like your generals do. They don't give a damn if you die. Your duty doesn't mean anything. You have a duty to yourself.*

It's reasonable to think such things. They make sense. And if people really were pawns and human affairs moved like chess, it might be an adequate story. Gallows humor is a time-honored trick for quelling such worries. I once had a Marine who would joke before doing anything dangerous, "If I die, make sure my company commander gets a ribbon!" But the thoughts easily fester. Whether spoken by Thersites or Barker, it doesn't really matter. That they're said aloud gives them unwarranted life. Wars can be lost for less.

Fortunately, the small man of the mind only tells part of the story. Odysseus beat Thersites with the royal scepter and rebuked him in front of all the troops. Captain Shinn did the same to Barker, reminding him of all the lion stood for, neutralizing the poison before it could spread through the team. But it was important that he didn't do it by simply getting Barker off the team or ordering him to go on watch. Shinn instead introduced the lion as a lawyer.

This was far beyond Neanderthal Logic or telling Barker he needed to shut up to get with the program. Shinn was inviting us to look at the lion under a microscope. Barker's argument was reasonable, but so was Shinn's. Shinn was just showing that there was a friendlier, more forgiving intelligence. The lion and the small man together could beat either the small man or the lion alone.

NOTHING MEANS ANYTHING

You can't be a king without sometimes doing what's ruthless. But when people see you acting ruthlessly, they'll tend to guard against you and look for opportunities to replace you. That's Machiavelli 101.

Shinn had shown me how a friendly and forgiving intelligence could still have teeth. But Those sorts of showdowns could only be won when the facts were on his side. Princes have plenty of other edge cases that need smoothing over. That's where Falstaff comes in.

In his philosophy, he doesn't need facts because nothing has any meaning. He embraces the cynical worldview, but comes to a very different conclusion than Jaques. Things don't actually add up. All the good we claim to do is just theater for those in power. But if that's the case, then you're free to do whatever you want. If it looks ugly, just use words to dress it up into something apparently noble. The difference between a gang member and a hedge fund manager is just that one wears a suit and tie.

Hal, besides being smart, is in a position that allows him to take these lessons in. After all, he's the heir apparent, a royal prince. But he hasn't always been a prince. That only came along when his father stole the crown. So what is this title? And furthermore, what good does it do you during a civil war that might unseat your father? If he dies, you won't be prince anymore. In that case, it doesn't mean anything good to be the prince—it means you'll be executed. That's a frightening and precarious position for a young man to be in. Falstaff can help with that.

Falstaff teaches Hal to be playful with giving things their meaning. Stealing is hard work that gives a man value, so let's call it a vocation. A pillow can become a crown if we place it on a prince's head. Hal, the son of a noble, can become a prince if his dad kills the king. Falstaff can be a knight, or a judge, or a hangman. Why not? It's just playing dress-up; it's all just fun.

The lion of the soul is appalled by this kind of play, but these are important lessons to understand if you're trying to reach positions of influence. Every lieutenant in the Marine Corps understands that he needs to find the right way to present what might have been a meaningless mission. That's why they present their commanders with things like: "Conducted 300 combat patrols." Did you accomplish anything on those patrols? Did we need 300 patrols? It doesn't matter. It sounds like a lot! That's a good lieutenant. Promote above peers.

Falstaff understands this wisdom deeply. His response is that you can't take any of it too seriously and you need to be able to playfully dress things up. Finding the right joke at the right time has gotten more than one president off the hook. In politics, you may not be able to change the facts, but you can always change the angle. We created a bloated agency that doesn't need to exist? Maybe, but we created thousands of jobs!

For Hal to navigate the only partially coherent landscape of his broken world, this is a skill he'll need in spades.

BANISHING TURNER

I had to learn to make ruthless moves with a bit of humor in Afghanistan. Turner and I had become buddies early on in our training. We were both new lieutenants thrilled to deploy. But in Afghanistan, we responded much differently to our mission. As my unanticipated admiration for Captain Shinn grew, I became his apprentice, giving everything I had to our mission. Turner for his part grew increasingly cynical. He was even starting to sound like Captain Barker.

I continued to stand up for Turner, feeling a sense of loyalty as his friend. But he became harder and harder to defend. He'd show up late for meetings and wouldn't complete assigned tasks. He would only engage with the Afghans socially, no longer working toward our team's mission. He'd be openly hostile, proclaiming that everything we did was useless.

Other teammates, now warmer to me, would ask me

what Turner's problem was. As I defended Turner, I began to resent him. In trying to be a good friend, I was becoming a bad leader. I was letting the mission and our morale suffer. I begged Turner to consider how he looked to the team, but he refused. I didn't know what to do.

Then, early one morning, I was still asleep in my tent when I heard my radio call, "Tent 2, Tent 2, this is Turner." All the team radios were on the same channel, allowing us transparent communication. Turner, I remembered, was up early to get breakfast with the Afghan logistics officer.

"Tent 2, Tent 2. Lieutenant Turner," the radio called again. I heard the staff sergeants rustle in their tent. Everyone was asleep, but Turner's call was slowly waking them up. *Damnit, Turner,* I thought. *Do you think about anyone other than yourself?* Tent 2 was the callsign of the tent where the translators slept. It seemed that Turner had forgotten to get his translator before he'd gone to meet the Afghans and decided to wake everyone up on the radio rather than running over to Tent 2. For some reason, Tent 2 wasn't responding. By the worry in his voice, it seemed that he was meeting the Afghans soon. "Tent 2! Tent 2! This is Turner!"

I'd had enough. I picked up my radio. "Go for Tent 2!" I yelled, doing my best impression of a translator's broken English.

"Finally," Turner came back. "Tent 2, I need Nuri to meet me at the gate right away."

"There is no Murray here, sir. Over," I replied, continuing my impression. I heard the staff sergeants turn up the volume on the radio. The whole team was listening.

"Murray?!" Turner yelled back. "Nuri! My translator."

"Ohhhhh, I see, sir," I replied, still mocking the translators' accent. "Stand by. Over."

"I can't stand by!" Turner was losing his patience quickly. "The logistics officer is walking over to me right now and I don't have a translator! Send. Nuri." I wanted to help him, but decided he needed some tough love. Humor had become my tool to handle sensitive leadership issues. Mean trick or not, I was doing my best to be a leader to the team.

"Sir," I called back, deciding I'd made my point. "Nuri is grumpy if I wake him again, sir. You must wake him, sir. Over and out."

The radio show was over, but the play continued. The whole team was awake now, having listened to the exchange. They now heard Turner jogging over to Tent 2, which turned out to be less than a minute from where he was standing. I, along with the entire team, wondered why he hadn't just jogged over in the first place. We listened through our tent walls as Turner unzipped the translators' tent to find 12 translators fast asleep. He didn't notice that their radio battery was dead.

"Are you kidding me?!" Turner screamed. "You're all asleep? Nuri! Get the hell out of your bed, get dressed, and come with me! We have breakfast this instant! Who was manning the radio?!!" We listened as Turner berated the tent of translators and they tried to defend themselves. Their weak English only served to confuse the situation further, as did Turner's wrongly assumed authority as he threatened to have them fired. The staff sergeants' laughter could be heard far outside their tent. I heard laughter from the captains' tent too.

No one was confused that I'd been ruthless and

calculating, but the prank served to smooth it over with laughs. They all knew after that moment that Turner was essentially cut from the team. But by making it look like a prank, I had a fig leaf to hide behind. I was able to cut Turner off without having to admit to anyone that that's what I did, or without having to openly talk about Turner's weaknesses. When anyone from the team would ask about it, I'd tell them it was only a joke.

Cutting my ties with Turner had been a relief to the team, but I was tortured by it. Shinn and I didn't talk much about it. "Cold-blooded . . ." he said with a grin when he saw me. Then we got back to work.

THE COLD EDGE OF COMMAND

Imbuing England with meaning, coherence, and purpose again was no easy or pleasant task. After usurping the crown, Bolingbroke had ruled over an all but broken kingdom, fragmented in speech and losing its respect for law. It was as though the upheaval and its illegitimacy had taken England backward into Hobbes's state of nature, in which culture and society don't exist, all is fear and violence, and human life is "solitary, poor, nasty, brutish, and short."

Whorehouses, thieves, and a surrender to bodily pleasure took center stage. In the two *Henry IV* plays, some of the nobles are of course very concerned with who wears the crown, but most of the characters just want politics out of their lives. There are always a few whose desire is to rule over others, while the many want to be simply left to themselves.

The singing and dancing, the friendly fellowship in the world of peasants and commoners, stands in stark contrast with the dark, somber chambers of the nobles' plotting. Hal has lived in both worlds. His princely task is to connect them and restore some health to the whole.

But both commoners and nobles have their own expectations of how that should go and what Hal should be doing as king. Once news breaks that Bolingbroke has died and that Hal has become King Henry V, Falstaff immediately begins to celebrate, believing that he will now rule England alongside Hal: "The laws of England are at my commandment," he yells. "Blessed are they that have been my friends; and woe to my lord chief justice!" Like all tyrants, his first thought is that he can commit crimes, helping his friends and punishing his enemies as he pleases. This is exactly what peasants and nobles alike fear in Hal's becoming king.

As Falstaff chases after the new king on his first procession, he's characteristically unpolitic in his approach. Hal, now playing the most serious game of dress-up in his life, is publicly showing himself for the first time as king. It's there that Falstaff shouts after him, "God save thy grace, King Hal! My royal Hal!" It's as if Thomas Jefferson's fat childhood friend had attended his inauguration, yelling, "President Tommy! Let's run the country together!" Everyone is all eyes to see how Hal will respond.

Hal is in a difficult position. Politically, it's absurd to have Falstaff at court. Just as the selfish buffoon had abandoned his troops to their death when he was a captain in the civil war, he could never be relied upon to look first to England's interests. On a personal level, though, Falstaff is the closest thing to a friend that Hal has in the world, and Hal understands better than most that politics isn't everything. The part of Hal that likes to drink with friends, play pranks, and banter has Falstaff for teacher and mentor. But as the king, Hal is pressed to renounce all those personal delights and satisfactions. Falstaff's impertinent appeal puts Hal on the spot of having to publicly formalize his decision to play the king.

"I know thee not, old man," Hal says to Falstaff in a line that's delivered like a bullet. He then proceeds to end their friendship harshly and decisively, banishing Falstaff from his presence on pain of death. He makes clear to all those listening that he is not the young prince he once was, that he is now a commanding king who will uphold the law. King Henry V of England will not be King Hal. His purely personal pleasures are cast aside along with Falstaff. As he'd long ago hinted, and as Falstaff had feared, Hal would indeed banish Falstaff and banish all his world.

Following this exchange, Falstaff will plunge into a deep depression and eventually die offstage, presumably from heartbreak. As king, Hal will sentence several of his old time friends to death when they're caught committing crimes. Like Richard and Bolingbroke before him, Hal will frequently wonder at the crushing weight of the crown and the sacrifice of private satisfaction that it demands.

Hal can see through the fanfare and frills that come with a leadership position. He sees behind the curtain. When people get close to power, they often report losing their awe and sometimes their respect. Many employees have heard me pitch my companies and rolled their eyes. They hear my pride of the past and optimism for the future, but they know all the current problems we're dealing with. When they see the whole picture, it leaves them bitter and angry.

But not Hal. Hal sees through the crown, the parades, and the ceremonies, yet he can still play along. Like Jaques, he sees that it's a stage, but he's excited to act on it, to bring life to the role of king. That role demands that he can no longer have a loudmouth thief as his counselor and friend. His commitment is what supports his power. It's not just acting.

Chapter 9

THE PRINCE BECOMES A KING

MOONLIGHTING

After the Marine Corps, I briefly worked at Morgan Stanley as an investment banker. Michael Grimes, a legend in investment banking, led our group. He was an inspiration to me in the power of playing a role well. He cemented the lesson of how playful sacrifice and acting could pull ahead of the cynical competition.

While I was there, Grimes got a meeting with Uber. His plan was to pitch Uber on going public, which would be a major win for Morgan Stanley both in profits and prestige. He directed two teams to work on the preparation separately so that he could pick the best aspects of each for his meeting.

It seemed cool to me, so I went to one of the team leaders hoping to join, but I was warned away. "No one wants to be on these teams," the leader told me. "Michael barely got a meeting with Uber and it's definitely not about an IPO. He's just making us do all of this for a minuscule chance they'll be interested." I was disappointed. I'd hoped that Grimes would live up to the stories about him. But in the time I'd worked with him he mostly stayed in his office and allowed his subordinate leaders to develop by running the day-to-day.

The night before the meeting, I was working on a different project when I saw Grimes in a conference room well after midnight. He was alone with his presentation pulled up as he practiced his pitch aloud. Grimes had already made himself a legend in banking. He was already rich. And still, there he was practicing like it was his big shot, staying up all hours to perfect it. I was amazed by his dedication, but it was nothing compared to what I learned of him the next day.

After the meeting, everyone in the office was talking about Grimes's presentation. It may have been a throwaway meeting when Uber scheduled it, but Grimes had been preparing long before the meeting. It turned out that Grimes had been moonlighting as an Uber driver himself for years! He had photos of himself with a driver's cap on and screenshots from his Uber profile.

He'd known that they would someday look to IPO, so he went to learn their business as deeply as he could. He went into the meeting knowing exactly how their business worked, what issues it had, and how it should be positioned to investors. He even had product suggestions to make the company better. When the Uber executives heard his pitch, they agreed to discuss an IPO with Morgan Stanley as the lead. When Uber went public, Morgan Stanley had won the deal.

The meeting turned out to be what the Marines call the "decisive opportunity," what Machiavelli calls the "Main Chance." What had looked to everyone else like a waste of time turned out to be exactly the right moment to summon all available combat power. This is what *thumos*, the lion, does best. He moves slowly, he sleeps, he stalks. But when the right gazelle makes the wrong move, the lion pounces, moving into a deep sprint until his prey is bloody before him.

NOT JUST FOX BUT LION TOO

Hotspur is the opposite of Falstaff. He is full of vigor, passion, and heart. He is an exemplar of courage on the battlefield, risking his life to kill the enemy in great numbers. He is quick to anger, especially when he sees something sacred being trampled on. In Richard's England, Hotspur would have been a happy knight, pleased to serve, fight, and die for his king and country. In Bolingbroke's England, he's disgusted with the apparent politician who has taken the rightful king's place, and he joins in a major uprising against him.

Though Hotspur leads rebels in a civil war, Shakespeare doesn't paint him as a straw man for Hal to knock down on the way to his throne. Not only is Hotspur gallant, he's also smart. He has a sharp tongue, is good to his wife, and can be very funny. As much as audiences find themselves on the fence about Hal, they tend to love Hotspur. Unlike Hal, Hotspur is who he is no matter the situation. He's a paragon of integrity.

Through all his vulgar jokes and dark threats, Hotspur is actually a decent man responding to indecent times.

From the very beginning, Hal and Hotspur are set as rivals when Bolingbroke, Hal's father, wishes out loud that Hotspur and Hal had been switched at birth, with Hotspur as his son all along. He longs for an heir as ambitious and valiant, so studious of honor and war; he's ashamed of a son who spends his time in bars and brothels, and who shows no interest in the doings of the court or the duties of a king. Bolingbroke has risked his life, his honor, and his country in taking the crown. Without a worthy successor, or at least an effective one, it will all have been in vain. Worse, he will have destroyed the England he loves.

Rivalry with Hotspur is a crucial element in Hal's carefully conceived plan for his kingship. In a famous soliloquy near the beginning of the play, he lets the audience in on his strategy of only pretending to be base and low. He considers it essential to his education. Furthermore, by being prepared to look so ugly, his glory will shine all the more beautifully when he emerges as a consummate king. Hotspur will continue to rack up his battle honors, but Hal believes he'll take them all when he defeats Hotspur in combat. The winning team doesn't need a perfect record; they only need to win the championship.

Henry IV, Part 1 is a play where the characters lie, get things wrong, and multiply the meanings of things. Unsurprisingly, Hal's plan doesn't come to fruition exactly as he imagined. Rather than going cleanly from disreputable teenager to glorious, commanding monarch, Hal is obliged to reveal his truer self, at least to his father, before he can orchestrate a final confrontation with Hotspur. He'll also later find himself waiting for an entire play as a prince ready to rule, waiting for his father to die. But first, Hal has to face Hotspur to repel the rebel forces.

His sword fight to the death with one of England's greatest warriors is a pivotal exam in Hal's strange education. Hal does kill Hotspur, but in leaving a corpse on the battlefield Hal means to take up all that Hotspur's soul had stood for. Though Hal never aimed to build his whole character around honor, as Hotspur did, he takes it far more seriously than Falstaff ever does, or could.

How the sword-fight scene gets played out is as varied as the directors putting on the show. To many, it looks like a blemish in the plot to have Hal beat Hotspur in single combat. We're told nothing of Hal's talent with a sword and never see him practicing or fighting, whereas we often hear of Hotspur's battle prowess.

Directors often add their own interpretation, making Hal play dirty somehow: throwing dirt in Hotspur's eyes or hitting him from behind. They can't imagine that Hal could so effectively summon the lion. But however Hal does it, his audience is forced to ponder how he could win such a fight without relying on Falstaffian tricks. We're forced to think about what else he's learned.

THE HONOUR OF SOLDIERS

If there was one place I expected to feel my inner lion roar, it was toward the Taliban. Novels and movies had convinced me that I'd be angry with the enemy, that our fight would feel personal. I thought this would be full *thumos* territory. When I imagined prisoners of war, I pictured knowing them from years of fighting and finally meeting them face-to-face. I envisioned walking into a windowless room with a hand in my pocket and sitting down in front of our prisoner. "Bet you never thought we'd find ourselves here," I'd say to him.

What I found instead was that the Afghans' prison resembled a cheap zoo. It was outside, walled-in with large mounds of dirt crowned with barbed wire. The prisoners slept in metal boxes the size of a small moving truck. I felt more administrative than I did angry.

One day, Monier, one of the Afghan soldiers I worked with, called me over to meet a man at their gate. He was an old man, respected in the community, but he'd come to plead for his son, whom the army had taken prisoner the day before. The father spoke of his mixed-up son with tears in his eyes, begging us to let him go. Although I felt for the father, I had no sympathy for his son.

John, my translator, and Monier led me to the son's holding cell. He was in a metal box, wearing swim goggles painted black. His face was badly cut, and his hands were bound with zip ties. Next to him was the five-gallon bucket he'd been given to relieve himself. The sight was disturbing; the smell was terrible. I'd never encountered anyone being treated so inhumanely. Yet, horrible as it was, I couldn't stop myself from wondering where the hell the Afghans had gotten swim goggles.

John asked the prisoner how long he'd been there. Eleven

days. Eleven days, deprived of sight, in 100-degree weather with next to no food and water, trading off the intensified heat of a metal can with the need for some shade. I looked at the man. He sat crumpled on the ground with his knees hugging his face and his arms hanging down like dead tree branches. He didn't want to be in the cage, but fury and resentment had passed. He wasn't trying to push through, or even hang on. It was resignation, despair, surrender.

Looked at from Jaques's harsh point of view, it might have seemed nothing more than an enemy being treated like an enemy. My mind might have calculated this as eye-for-an-eye justice, or rationalized that we needed to neutralize the threat. Instead, my lion was reacting. I was angry, but not at the prisoner.

I pulled Monier to the side. "Take his goggles off now," I ordered. "Get him out of that box, untie his hands, feed him, and give him water." John translated, but Monier didn't need the words. He understood my tone. I had no formal authority to order Monier. This was his prisoner in his prison. Still, he didn't hesitate and immediately started ordering the guards to fix the situation.

I hadn't expected that my lion would stand up for an enemy prisoner. But *thumos* has integrity at its foundation. I'd reflected a long time on something Churchill wrote: "One rule of conduct alone survives as a guide to men in their wanderings: fidelity to covenants, the honour of soldiers, and the hatred of causing human woe." When covenants are broken, soldiers act dishonorably, or someone takes pleasure in causing pain to humans, anger is the right response. The mind might rationalize that the ends justify the means. The hydra only cares that he's not the one feeling pain. But the lion steps up to defend.

WE HAPPY FEW

Shakespeare's education of Prince Hal combines the leonine temperament and conduct of Hotspur with the foxlike craft of Falstaff. But while Hal becomes a master of both, he also recognizes the limits of each alone. Through swings of fortune and shifting loyalties, Hal adapts like an actor—sometimes playing the fox, sometimes the lion—as he rises from prince to king.

Prince Hal's decisive achievement comes after he has killed Hotspur, banished Falstaff, and succeeded his father on the throne. *Henry V* begins with Hal as the reigning king, deciding whether to wage war on France. He does. After pushing into the heart of France, Hal arrives with his starving, greatly weakened army near Agincourt. His forces are outnumbered by the French five to one. The English army is on its last legs; the French soldiers are fresh.

Hal's men are awaiting all but certain death. Meanwhile, the confident French polish their armor and prepare for what they're sure will be a decisive victory. The night belongs to historical record, yet Shakespeare inserts a scene of his own: Hal dresses up as one of the common soldiers and tours the camp, speaking to his men in disguise. Their morale is worse than he'd imagined.

This is the first time we're given a clearer sense of just

how fragile Hal's enterprise is. One battle tomorrow, and his kingdom could easily be lost. All the long struggle of rebellion and civil war, all the plotting and scheming, all the risk, sacrifice, and compromise of the last 16 years will have been for naught, if it ends with France taking over England.

Hal's night of vigil ends in deep frustration. After taming and bending fortune to his will, after making himself an acute student of human nature and his subjects, high to low, and after putting all his honor at stake, the crown whose glory he has worked so hard to repair may yet be consigned to oblivion. As for his men, despite Hal's vision and inspired leadership, they remain skeptical, some even cynical.

In the dead of night, Hal delivers his last soliloquy. It's his longest speech. He has heard his soldiers speak of him as if he were something different, something higher, not quite a man like them. He curses ceremony, a word that hasn't been heard since *Richard II* when King Richard cursed the appearances that seemed to make him different from other men. This is Hal's low point: facing death, invisible to his countrymen, the unjust king who waged a losing war. He completes his speech with a prayer and the scene ends.

When next we see Hal, it's morning. He goes on to deliver perhaps the most famous battle speech of all time: "We few, we happy few, we band of brothers . . ." It so rouses his soldiers and excites them for battle that, despite the terrible odds, the English army triumphs. Their losses and casualties are miraculously low—only 29 English compared to 10,000 French. The victory brings France under Hal's rule. The overly confident French now surrender in full. They lay down their arms, beg Hal's mercy, negotiate the terms of relinquishing the French crown, and marry Hal to the French princess.

Hal's celebrated speech combines Hotspur's devotion to honor with Falstaff's embodiment of humor. The central reasoning of the speech is a joke about honor: The fewer the men, the greater each man's share of the honor will be. Hotspur had made the same joke earlier, but in much less weighty circumstances. "Wish not one man more," Hal exhorts his bedraggled, depleted army, as if they couldn't do with greater numbers to make the odds more even.

Like when the Marine general Chesty Puller, surrounded by the enemy, quipped that the bastards can't get away this time, Hal can be merry in the face of death. Falstaff and Hotspur represent two deep styles of response to the moral and spiritual disarray in England after Bolingbroke's seizure of the crown. One answered the upheaval with comedy, the other with courage.

Playful distance and valiant commitment show up as poles in Hotspur and Falstaff; Hal represents how they can work together. Just as Shakespeare's mix of comedies and tragedies makes audiences laugh and weep, shudder and rejoice, Falstaff and Hotspur touch and move men's hearts. One rouses armies; the other entertains taverns. Hotspur channels passion for honor as Falstaff lets his passions run free. Hal is master of both their arts, fusing them into an alloy of accomplished leadership that managed to turn a doomed army of his fellow Englishmen into a band of brothers who made history.

According to the textbooks, Henry's victory depended heavily on the longbow and the stakes deployed in defense against the French cavalry, as well as the mud and confinement of the battlefield. Shakespeare mentions none of that. Instead, he credits Hal's understanding of his army and how he spoke to them, appealing to their sense of honor along with their sense of humor. Arrows certainly did kill French soldiers, but it was English hearts that loosed them.

The Battle of Agincourt and Hal's celebrated Saint Crispin's Day speech show the lion in all its glory. It's a story we all know and love, the tale of a small but committed army defeating an outsized and overconfident enemy: David and Goliath once again. Yet Shakespeare couples the magnificent moment with his scene of Hal as fox. Hal's kingly roar is more richly understood when we've been shown all that fed into it and how some shadowy business in the night was an indispensable part of his doing glorious work in the daylight.

A WAR STORY

Near the end of our tour, the Afghans planned their first major operation. I was thrilled. For nearly a year, we'd joined them on small patrols that essentially looked for trouble. I'd never known them to have an actual mission or to mass their firepower. It sounded too good to be true.

As we prepared for the operation on the southern border of an enemy hotbed, I was amazed. The Afghan Army was partnered with the police. The religious and government leaders had signed off. The generals set up in a tent that had a large map on the table with pins in it to mark their troops' locations. I'd never seen them do anything like it.

When the operations started, John and I stayed with the

Afghan leaders every waking hour. We helped coordinate drones overhead, and Haberer acted as a liaison with Marine artillery to support them. There were bombs dropping and firefights in every direction. The Taliban was largely outnumbered, but they still put up a serious fight. Wounded soldiers would come back to be treated by the medical tent set up next to us. This was the real war.

For the entire year, I'd felt as though Afghanistan didn't represent a war at all. There seemed to be no front lines, no missions, no victories. But in this operation, a thousand Afghan soldiers all moved in the same direction for a shared purpose.

At one point, the Taliban waved a white flag as they drove a car through with a trunk full of dead bodies. The force known best for burying bombs and using civilians as shields actually waved a white flag. And no one thought of firing on them. I was shocked. I'd thought the white flag had gone out with Lobsterbacks and muskets. But here were the Taliban waving one while everyone on the battlefield respected it. I couldn't believe it, I was seeing the true honor of soldiers in a real battle over contested ground.

By the end of our operation, the Afghans had killed the Taliban resisters and built six police stations. We hadn't fought the battle for them, but supported and advised them. We'd completed our mission and built something good. It was unbelievable to me. A sudden game-winning grand slam after eight innings of a no-hitter.

Barker and the others laughed at my naivete. Sure, they conceded, we'd established police stations in an enemy stronghold, but how long before the police were bribed? All we'd achieved were dead bodies on both sides that amounted to nothing. We could dress it up and call it an achievement, but no good would come from the operation. We were organizing deck chairs on the *Titanic*. They saw the white flag as a barbarian's stop sign.

They may have been right about the final outcome. I have no doubt that 15 years later, the Taliban is running those police stations. But even if what they were saying sounded right, I knew that they weren't seeing the whole picture. They'd understood the ultimate utility of the operation, but they didn't see the beauty. They were blind to the matters of *thumos*.

When only paying attention to the mind, it can be easy to feel like nothing really matters in the end. We win the war by building a nuclear bomb, but now need to worry that we'll all blow ourselves into extinction. Yet even if our best achievements are sandcastles that won't make it through the tide, they bring some small meaning into the world, even if only for a little time.

As much as we may argue about the absolute goods of things, there's still a broad landscape we can agree on. Having police officers there was better than having drug runners. And as much as we may have improved Trek Nawa, no one on earth would choose it as their vacation spot. Things are never permanent or perfect on earth, but the better things are still worth fighting to build.

WHAT IF ANGER IS THE ANSWER?

I'd started out by seeing that anger with myself could be a tool to sculpt and shape my soul. As I went through Marine training and into Afghanistan, I began to develop some of the deeper skills and unexpected lessons involved. Marine training taught me that I needed friends and fellowship. Working with the Afghan Army showed me how to negotiate with strangers and to turn them into friends. Falstaff helped me understand how to use humor and playfulness to smooth over a necessary edginess. Then Henry V gave me an example of what it looked like when it all came together.

The anger that was so raw to begin with had turned into something princelike and commanding. The small man, the lion, and the hydra could all work together in one beautiful soul. I'd learned how to be Machiavellian without being heartless and how to be loyal without being stupid. And I'd learned to take satisfaction in all of its working together.

My adventure had started out with the hope of becoming an Achilles or a Hotspur, to dominate through excellence alone. Such a dream is always out there for the chasing. The ancients, the Bible, and the Renaissance all had those kinds of heroes. It seemed natural to want to become one.

It wasn't a bad goal. I wanted to be the best so that I could protect my country. I wanted to dedicate my life and work to protecting the things I loved. Those kinds of noble aspirations are easily written off as idealistic and, after a while, I started to think that too.

When I joined the Marines, I quickly found that I couldn't do it alone. Even more than that, I realized I didn't want to do it alone. As our team grew, I met all the strangers and weirdos you need to partner with if you want to get big. A coalition is an odd group. They weren't often trying to protect anything. They usually didn't have noble ends. They were either looking out for themselves or wanted something I didn't care about. But since we needed each other to succeed, we'd partner up. Big tents always turn into circuses.

And that's where most people end. Whatever their initial nobility, their careers get overrun by unpaid bills, tax questions, and acronyms they need to look up for the fifth time. The pure love they'd sought turns into dirty diapers, school lunches, and scheduling issues. And the excellence they'd once eagerly chased becomes doing things just well enough to get by. The world is no place for excellence, nobility, and heroes. Those are things for bedtime stories and romance novels. No one treats them seriously in the real world.

But as my own version of that cynicism started to set in, I'd also been exposed to new kinds of leadership and excellence. I'd begun thinking that the contest was simply to become the best and to rule the others. I came to find that political leadership was necessary to hold everything together.

Political leadership didn't seem as gloriously good as the excellence of the heroes I'd seen at first. Achilles is constantly hamstrung by Agamemnon, his general. Hotspur can't stand the politics of the king and gives his life to overthrow him. Political leaders might not look as splendid as Achilles, but they're far from any less important.

My favorite heroes seemed to need good lawyers. They worked in the dark when necessary, but triumphed in the light. They weren't perfect but often seemed to perform miracles. Leaders like Prince Hal are full souls. Through them, we see how our intelligence, desire, and aggression can work together to create something beautiful.

There's something wild, playful, and adaptive in those

princes. That means that sometimes they color outside of the lines. I think about them as God's headaches, the class clowns who will become captains of industry. Their stories aren't tidy. Yet their wildness is what gives these heroes the flexibility to connect and bring large groups together.

These princes teach a crucial lesson to anyone trying to build something in our broken world: Survive ambiguity and wait until fortunes turn. It's not the central lesson of this book, but it's worth underlining because it's very likely the next step you need to take. To me, this is the critical lesson that can help you build something even when you're most cynical.

This is what almost everyone gets wrong—especially smart people. Smart people don't like living with ambiguity. They want to talk things out and make a decision. "At the end of the day, it's either A or B," they say, smugly believing that their minds can fathom all possibilities. "We need to choose one soon."

But life doesn't work that way. The possibilities we see are usually banal versions of the strange reality that will soon emerge. Fortune is stranger than fiction. Weird things happen all the time, and you just never know when a car crash or a cancer diagnosis will change everything. New cards are dealt every day. You'd be a fool to think you need to go all in on the hand you're holding now.

Hal waited years to put on the crown after he was ready to become king. He didn't force things to a head. He waited. He watched. And when the right moment arrived, he pounced on it.

Many will go their whole lives not knowing quite what to

do with their anger. Many will subtly ignore honor and, with it courage, loyalty, and fellowship. Most will never engage in a real competition to be the best, and for many of those who do, they won't care how they win so long as they come out on top. Most of the people I see get too busy for an honor story. With kids, a marriage, a job, and dreams of success, it's hard to find time for nobility. But for a rare few, they'll find their greatest adventures begin with the conviction that nobility matters.

PART IV
RETROSPECTIVE

- An effective leader needs to balance between self-interested calculation (the cynic's view) and selfless nobility (a hero's view) (see "After Cynicism," page 171).
- Cynicism almost always makes sense. But cynicism is just smart, not wise. Merely making sense is inadequate (see "It Doesn't Make Sense," page 175).
- Don't just correct the argument. Show the beautiful thing that's missing (see "It Doesn't Make Sense," page 175).
- In politics, you may not be able to change the facts, but you can always change the angle (see "Nothing Means Anything," page 180).
- Humor is a crucial tool to keep you nimble enough to handle ambiguity (see "Banishing Turner," page 182).

- There's a way to master cynicism: Integrate it but refuse to collapse into it. Understand what's ugly but use it in service of the beautiful (see "After Cynicism," page 171).
- Cynicism can't be suppressed—it must be answered and reframed, or it will rot the team from within (see "It Doesn't Make Sense," page 175).
- Meanings are malleable, but that doesn't make life meaningless. You can shape meaning (see "Nothing Means Anything," page 180).
- When the world is absurd, don't despair. Laugh—and then make it yours (see "Nothing Means Anything," page 180).
- You may need to make personal sacrifices to play the role you want in life (see "The Cold Edge of Command," page 185).
- When your big opportunity comes, you need to give it all your efforts and resources (see "Moonlighting," page 189).
- Loyalty doesn't look like it makes sense. Neither does courage. Yet both are more beautiful responses (see "Trust and Loyalty," page 162).
- Honor needs to be taken seriously, but when we seek it without a sense of humor, we become tragic figures (see "Not Just Fox but Lion Too," page 191).
- The best princes and leaders act like foxes on some occasions (avoiding traps) and like lions at other times (standing up and fighting). You may need detailed strategy sessions before making a good presentation, or you may need to do a lot of planning before you have a great

date with someone (see "Not Just Fox but Lion Too," page 191).

- Even if our best achievements are sandcastles that won't make it through the tide, they bring some small meaning into the world, even if only for a moment (see "A War Story," page 199).
- Survive ambiguity and wait until fortunes turn (see "What If Anger Is the Answer?," page 201).

Coda: Another Letter to My Son

Dear Michael,

I'm not sure if you remember, but when you were eight years old, you smoked a cigar with me and Benedict in our backyard. At the time, you didn't know how to take the smoke in your mouth, so I'd hold it up to your lips and you'd blow smoke out of it. I remember thinking that cigars don't actually need to be smoked to invite a feeling of manly sophistication and reflection.

Benedict was only 12 at the time, and this was his first cigar. Aunt Kelly warned him that he'd get sick, but he didn't care. He was so excited. We could see the ocean and the stars that night. He had a look on his face like he was getting away with murder.

Benedict asked me what it was like in war. You kept reminding me what stories I should tell him. Most of those stories are in this book. You imagined yourselves there, told me what you would have done in my position. Uncle Ian had died three years before, but I know he would have smiled to see us smoking our cigars and telling war stories.

It was almost 20 years before that Ian had come home with me to Ohio for the summer to paint houses. We'd met in college and obsessed over Plato and Shakespeare together. He'd had his first taste of leadership on the soccer field in high school and he loved hearing about the leadership I was learning while we painted houses each summer. He wanted to learn too.

Throughout the days, we'd work hard, carrying ladders and painting walls. Most of the nights, we were so exhausted by the time we got home that we would go straight to sleep. But some nights, we'd stay up talking with my dad.

Grandpa John has the best stories. He'd tell us how he started painting houses when he was 17 because he made a decision that he'd never work for anyone else. About how he started to build his crew of painters, how he'd motivate and teach them. He'd tell stories about when he hired more and more people, how revenues went up but so did stress. He told us how his profits went down. He told us about when his two best painters threatened a coup, and how he dispatched their plot. How his accountant and friend stole from him. And how he managed to run that business for over 50 years.

My dad's stories took place in the Ohio suburbs. Mine took place in a war in Afghanistan. And although we were different generations telling different stories, the themes remained much the same.

They were stories of breaking off on our own, sick of being

told what to do. They were stories about us earning our spurs and having to decide what to do once we won them. About how we started alone but found friends and allies along the way. About growing our teams until they were ready to burst. At times, they were stories about betrayal, coups, and tricks, but they were about loyalty and mercy too. Wherever our stories took place, they all ended the same way, with us building something solid out of broken parts.

Nights like those have been around as long as fathers and sons. They're an ancient oral tradition passed down from generation to generation. They start as entertainment. They become our maps for how we navigate from boyhood to becoming men.

I don't know your stories yet. I don't know if they'll be set in the suburbs or perhaps in space. I don't know the characters who will join you, the hardships you'll suffer, or the triumphs you'll enjoy. But I do know that they'll echo the themes you've heard before, that you'll build something you're proud of, and that through it you'll become a man.

I don't know how those stories will go, but I can't wait to hear you tell them.

Love,
Dad

Acknowledgments

This book started as a 200,000-word journal I'd kept while I was in Afghanistan. What I wrote down there is the big block of marble out of which family, friends, and many other supporters helped me chisel and shape into what you now have in your hands.

My mom, dad, and brother, Matthew, contributed to every draft, but their help started long before I began writing. When I was a kid, my family read hundreds of books together. We had so much fun doing it that I only had two dreams for my life: to write a book and to start a family. They worked with me on this book like they used to help me with my essays in school. Every vignette is also now what we called the "Matthew version," after he helped me understand how to frame the stories to make better sense.

Michael was our only kid when I started writing this

book, but as Claire and Ellie were born, they all became my ideal readers. I imagined the three of them as young adults sitting across the desk from me as I wrote. My over-arching goal was to make something that could be useful to them someday. By the time they were six, seven, and eight, they had often requested these as their bedtime stories.

I owe so much to my teachers, mentors, and friends. In school: Sallie Fine, my high school English teacher, who convinced me to go to college and to study the Greeks; Mera Flaumenhaft, who opened up *As You Like It* and the Old Testament to me; Zdravko Planinc, who helped me understand *Hamlet*; Victor Davis Hanson, who taught me about Thucydides and Plutarch; and, most of all, my friend and former professor, Carl Page, who helped me understand Plato, Aristotle, Homer, Machiavelli, *Richard II*, Prince Hal, and my own mind as well. I worked closely on every vignette with Carl and owe him a great deal for his help and wisdom.

In the Marines: Lee Shinn, Tom Schueman, and Phil Treglia, who together shaped me into a Marine Leader; Jeremiah Johnson, Mike Lones, George Harvey, and Jake Vreeland, for helping me to understand the core concepts of this book; LtGen George Smith (ret.) and MajGen Bill Seely (ret.), who trained me as a Marine and set an impossible standard for me to strive for; Tim and Sandy Day, who have shown me what it means to serve once I was out of uniform; and the Tim Day Tribe for helping me reflect on Marine leadership throughout my writing. Special thanks to Tom Schueman, Rye Barcott, Steven Pressfield, Karl Marlantes, Nate Fick, and Vice President J. D. Vance for talking to me about what it means to write a book as a Marine.

In Harvard and business: Sabrina Castenfelt, who convinced Chiryze and me that I should write a book; Jonathan "JCron" Cronstadt, who showed me how to sell it; Jeffrey Rayport, who introduced frameworks that change the way I think; David Fubini, who helped me develop my thoughts on leadership; Bob White, who offered feedback and helped me communicate some of the harder ideas; Adi Ignatius, who helped me develop the idea and introduced me to a long list of Harvard alumni who weighed in; Alfred Lin and Carl Eschenbach, for helping me understand how to use what I learned in the Marines as a founder; David Cahn, who helped me understand that aggression is a virtue in tech founders; and Sankaet Pathak, who exemplifies how the lion and the small man can work together.

Thanks to Charlie Fusco for my title, proposal, and helping to turn it into something someone might want to read. Thanks to Charlie Walk for helping me understand how to position the book. And thanks to Matt Holt, Katie Dickman, and the whole BenBella team for helping me make major improvements to my manuscript and getting it out to the world.

Also thanks to Ian Lindquist, Kelly Lindquist-Ray, Lisa Lindquist, Ted Lindquist (really, all the Lindquists except for Garth), Cathy White, Paul Wilford, Andrew Romiti, Ben Gringeri, Michael Foley, Marci Tatham, Matt Tatham, Chris Mallard, Ghanim Marouf, Bridgette Wensel, Lauren Mayfield, Pouya Hashemi, Caren Utino, Tiffany Hill, and Chad Twiggs for their input on different sections.

Finally, thanks to my wonderful wife, Chiryze, who was my biggest supporter and harshest critic. Chiryze was the one who pushed me to write this book and then helped me through the next eight years I worked on it. She took care of our three babies at 5 AM so that I could write for a few hours before work each day. When I got rejected by publishers, she told me they were idiots. Whenever I wanted to give up, she'd tell me that we don't give up on lifelong dreams. So much of the credit for this book, for my companies, and for my happiness belongs to her.

About the Author

Photo by Mac Kotas

Mike LeBlanc is a decorated Marine Corps major, Harvard Business School graduate, and a unicorn founder in Silicon Valley. He is the cofounder of Foundation Future Industries, a defense-focused robotics company building humanoid robots for the Department of Defense, and the cofounder of Cobalt Robotics, a Silicon Valley startup backed by Sequoia, Founders Fund, and Coatue (acquired in 2024). With 13 years of service in the Marine Corps, LeBlanc deployed three times to the Middle East and served as an economic and technology advisor to the Pentagon. His leadership and strategic vision have been featured in *The Wall Street Journal*, *Newsweek*, *Fast Company*, and *Business Insider* and on *NBC Nightly News* and CNBC.